WHO
IS GOD?

Michael Jackson, D.D.
Cecilia Jackson, D.D.

ISBN: 9798631325838

Scripture quotation from the King James Translation.

Produced in the United States through "I AM" Productions.

"Who Is God," is a systematic bible
study that leads individuals into relationship
with Christ and establishing the foundation
that is required in order to mature in Him.

"And ye shall know
[understand, comprehend, be completely aware of]
the truth, and the **TRUTH** shall
make you free." John 8:32

Dedicated to all those who are the
"Church within the Church"
in this latter day movement who sincerely
want to **KNOW** the **TRUTH** of God
without all the "trappings" of
present day Christianity.

May the Holy Spirit **"open"** your eyes as **He did ours ...**

WHO IS GOD?

Table of Contents

Chapter 1
THE BIBLE TO THE DISCIPLE

1. WHAT IS THE BIBLE?

☐ The Bible is a book written by the motivation of God. Disciples receive this book as God's words recorded on paper.

• "All scripture is given by inspiration of God."2 Timothy 3:16

2. WHO RECORDED THE WORDS OF GOD?

☐ God's holy men, inspired in their hearts by the Spirit of God, recorded the words of God. This makes the Bible different from any other book. God influenced their thoughts as they wrote the words dictated (given) from God.

• "...Holy men of God spake as they were moved by the Holy Ghost.." 2 Peter 1:21.

• "We speak, not in the words which man's wisdom teacheth, but which the Holy Ghost teacheth." 1 Corinthians 2:13.

3. WHY IS IT SO IMPORTANT FOR US TO HAVE THE BIBLE?

☐ God wanted us to have a record of his words so that we may read them and be led to Christ. The whole book speaks of Christ. God used the prophets to write the Old Testament. In the New Testament he used his apostles.

☐ We also realize Christ as the fulfillment of the Old Testament through the preaching and teaching of God's followers in the New Testament.

• "Search the scriptures; for in them ye think ye have eternal life: and they are they which testify of me." John 5:39.

> • "Then said I, Lo, I come: in the volume of the book it is written of me." Psalms 40:7.

4. WHAT ARE THE MAIN TEACHING CATEGORIES OF THE BIBLE?

☐ There are two main teaching categories of the Bible, the Law and the Gospel.

☐ The Law was given to God's leader, Moses. It was to teach God's people to obey him, to show them how to live good lives, and to show them characteristics of sin through knowing the law. The Law is the Ten Commandments, which serves to show mankind that he still needs to be brought into a relationship with Christ.

> • "...For by the law is the knowledge of sin." Romans 3:20.

> • "Wherefore the law was our schoolmaster to bring us unto Christ, that we might be justified by faith." Galatians 3:24.

☐ The Gospel is the portion of the scripture that tells of the gift of salvation through Jesus Christ. It is the Word of God that presents deliverance and hope to man.

> • "In this was manifested the love of God toward us, because that God sent his only begotten Son into the world that we might live through him." 1 John 4:9.

5. WHAT IS THE BIBLE TO US TODAY?

☐ The Bible is a roadmap or guide to salvation in Jesus Christ for us today. It helps us to know, have faith in, love, and walk in the ways of Christ. Therefore we need to read it daily that we may be steered, by God, in the right direction.

• "So then faith cometh by hearing, and hearing by the word of God." Romans 10:17.

• "Thy word is a lamp unto my feet and a light unto my path." Psalms 119:105.

6. WHAT HAPPENS WHEN WE READ THE BIBLE?

☐ When we read the Bible our minds are changed from our old way of thinking to the way Christ wants us to think. Once we learn to think the way He thinks, we respond the way He would respond in situations. The process of changing our minds by reading God's word is described in the scripture as changing our carnal minds into spiritual minds.

• "For to be carnally minded is death: but to be spiritually minded is life and peace. Because the carnal mind is enmity against God: for it is not subject to the law of God, neither indeed can be. So then they that are in the flesh cannot please God." Romans 8:6-8.

7. DO I NEED TO BECOME FAMILIAR WITH THE BOOKS OF THE BIBLE?

☐ Yes. All Disciples need to be familiar with the Bible and need to know by memory the books of the Bible. Since the Bible is our roadmap through life and truth in every matter, we need to know how to find scripture verses quickly and easily. Memorize them in this order.

• Old Testament (Historical Books): Genesis, Exodus, Leviticus, Numbers, Deuteronomy, Joshua, Judges, Ruth, 1 Samuel, 2 Samuel, 1 Kings, 2 Kings, 1 Chronicles, 2 Chronicles, Ezra, Nehemiah, Esther, Job, Psalms, Proverbs, Ecclesiastes, Song of Solomon, Isaiah, Jeremiah, Ezekiel, Lamentations, Daniel, Hosea, Joel, Amos, Obadiah, Jonah, Micah, Nahum, Habakkuk, Zephaniah, Haggai, Zechariah, Malachi

• New Testament (Historical): Matthew, Mark, Luke, John, Acts, Romans, 1 Corinthians, 2 Corinthians, Galatians, Ephesians, Philippians, Colossians, 1 Thessalonians, 2 Thessalonians, 1 Timothy, 2 Timothy, Titus, Philemon, Hebrews, James, 1 Peter, 2 Peter, 1 John, 2 John, 3 John, Jude, Revelation

Chapter 2
ALPHA

8. DID GOD HAVE AN ORIGIN?

☐ There is no beginning or ending with God. God is eternal. Before anything ever was ... God Is. Even before there was any idea of time, God existed. The scripture says that God is the Alpha and Omega, the beginning and the ending. (Revelation 21:6-7).

> • "Lord, thou hast been our dwelling place in all generations. Before the mountains were brought forth, or ever thou hadst formed the earth and the world, even from everlasting to everlasting, thou art God." Psalms 90:1-2.

9. HOW MAY I UNDERSTAND GOD BEING ETERNAL AND HAVING NO BEGINNING?

☐ It helps to understand God's infinite (forever) existence by knowing that God is Spirit. This means he is intelligent and totally free (cannot be confined). Because he has no body, he cannot be destroyed.

> • "Now unto the King eternal, immortal, invisible, the only wise God, be honour and glory for ever and ever. Amen." 1 Timothy 1:17.

> • "A spirit hath not flesh and bones." Luke 24:39.

10. WHAT ARE SOME OTHER TRUTHS THE BIBLE REVEALS ABOUT GOD?

☐ The Bible reveals that God is love, light, and life. The scriptures reveal that He is one God, without partiality (meaning he is fair and just), He has knowledge of all things, He is almighty, He is in every place all in the same time. Without sin, He is holy.

• HE KNOWS ALL THINGS: "O Lord, thou hast searched me and known me. Thou knowest my downsittings and mine uprisings; thou understandest my thought afar off. Thou compassest my path and my lying down and art acquainted with all my ways.  For there is not a word in my tongue, but, O Lord, thou knowest it altogether." Psalms 139:1-4.

• LIGHT: "God is light and in him is no darkness at all." 1 John 1:5.

• LOVE: "God is love." 1 John 4:8.

• SPIRIT: "God is a spirit." John 4:24.

• HE SEES EVERYTHING: "The eyes of the Lord are in every place, beholding the evil and the good." Proverbs 15:3.

• HE IS WITHOUT INIQUITY: "A God of truth and without iniquity, just and right is he." Deuteronomy 32:4.

Chapter 3
THE IDENTITIES OF GOD

11. HOW IS ALL OF THE WORK OF GOD TO BE UNDERSTOOD SINCE GOD IS ONE GOD?

☐ Even though God is one, we must understand that in God there are three distinct identities - the Father, Son, and Holy Spirit. The scriptures below demonstrates these three divine identities:

• "And Jesus [The Son] when he was baptized, went up straightway out of the water: and lo, the heavens were open to him, and he saw the Spirit of God [The Holy Spirit] descending like a dove, and lighting upon him; And lo a voice from heaven, [God the Father] saying, This is my beloved Son, in whom I am well pleased." Matthew 3:16-17.

12. HOW DO I MAKE A DISTINCTION BETWEEN THE THREE DIVINE IDENTITIES?

☐ Here is a simple distinction between the three identities of God, we credit: 1) the work of creation to God the Father; 2) the work of redemption (deliverance) to the Son Jesus Christ; 3) and the work of sanctification (purification) to the Holy Spirit.

• "In the beginning God [the Father] created the heaven and the earth." Genesis 1:1.

• "But when the fullness of the time was come, God sent forth his Son [Jesus] made of a woman, made under the law, To redeem them that were under the law, that we might receive the adoption of sons." Galatians 4:4-5.

• "Elect according to the foreknowledge of God the Father, through sanctification of the [Holy] Spirit, unto obedience and sprinkling of the blood of Jesus Christ: Grace unto you, and peace, be multiplied." 1 Peter 1:2.

13. HOW IS IT THAT THESE THREE DISTINCT IDENTITIES ARE ONE?

☐ God chose to reveal himself to us through Jesus Christ and the Holy Spirit. They are all of the same substance for they come forth (function) from God Himself.

☐ To understand this truth, consider the fact that a woman could function as a mother, and function also as a wife, and be a sister, and still be someone's daughter, and have a career or serve as a nurse. Though she functions in all of these roles, she is yet one substance one person. Use this same concept to understand the identities of God; then you will be able to better understand that when we reach heaven we will see only ONE God.

• "In the beginning was the Word, and the Word was with God and the Word was God." John 1:1.

• "Hear, O Israel: The Lord our God is one Lord." Deuteronomy 6:4.

• [Jesus speaking] "That they may be ONE, as WE are one." John 17:11.

14. IS THE ONENESS OF GOD A TRUTH PEOPLE STRUGGLE WITH TODAY?

☐ Yes. The oneness of God is one of the greatest controversial issues in the body of Christ and in the world today.

• "And without controversy great is the mystery of godliness: God was manifest in the flesh, justified in the Spirit, seen of angels, preached unto the Gentiles, believed on in the world, received up into Glory." 1 Timothy 3:16.

15. HAS GOD REVEALED HIMSELF IN OTHER FORMS TO MAN?

☐ Yes. God has revealed himself to man in various forms listed below:

• A Cloud: "And the Lord went before them by day in a pillar of a cloud, to lead them the way; and by night in a pillar of fire, to give them light; to go by day and night: He took not away the pillar of the cloud by day, nor the pillar of fire by night, from before the people." Exodus 13:21-22.

• The Angel of the Lord: "And an angel of the Lord came up from Gilgal to Bochim, and said, I made you to go up out of Egypt, and have brought you unto the land which I sware unto your fathers; and I said, I will never break my covenant with you." Judges 2:1.

• The Rock: "And did all drink the same spiritual drink; for they drank of that spiritual Rock that followed them; and that Rock was Christ." 1 Corinthians 10:4.

• As His Shekkinah Glory: "And he said, I beseech thee, show me thy glory. And he said, I will make all my goodness pass before thee, and I will Proclaim the name of the LORD before thee; and will be gracious to whom I will be gracious, and will show mercy on whom I will show mercy. And he said, Thou canst not see my face: for there shall no man see me, and live. And the LORD said, Behold, there is a place by me, and thou shalt stand upon a rock: And it shall come to pass, while my glory passeth by, that I will put thee in a clift of the rock, and will cover thee with my hand while I pass by: And I will take away mine hand, and thou shalt see my back parts: but my face shall not be seen." Exodus 33:18-23

• As the God Man Jesus Christ: "In the beginning was the Word, and the Word was with God, and the Word was God. The same was in the beginning with God. All things were made by him; and without him was not any thing made that was made ... And the Word was made flesh, and dwelt among us, (and we beheld his glory, the glory as of the only begotten of the Father,) full of grace and truth." John 1:13-14

•As the Holy Spirit: "And it shall come to pass afterward, that I will pour out my spirit upon all flesh; and your sons and your daughters shall prophesy, your old men shall dream dreams, your young men shall see visions." Joel 2:28

Chapter 4
HAVE YOU EVER HEARD OF ANGELS?

16. WHAT ARE ANGELS?

☐ Angels are spiritual beings created by God with more intelligence and power than man. They have been given a free will to serve and obey God. They are spirit beings created by God for the purpose of worshiping and serving Him eternally. Should they choose to disobey God there is no forgiveness or salvation provided for them.

• "But one in a certain place testified, saying, What is man, that thou art mindful of him? or the son of man, that thou visitest him? Thou madest him a little lower than the angels; thou crownedst him with glory and honour, and didst set him over the works of thy hands." Hebrews 2:6-7

• "Bless the Lord, ye his angels, that excel in strength, that do his commandments, hearkening unto the voice of his word. Bless ye the Lord, all ye his hosts; ye ministers of his, that do his pleasure." Psalms 103:20-21

• ". . . Thousand thousands ministered unto him, and ten thousand times ten thousand stood before him. . ." Daniel 7:10

17. SINCE ANGELS ARE SPIRIT BEINGS CAN THEY BECOME VISIBLE?

☐ Yes. Angels can become visible. They are a spirit and not

limited to physical confines. There are many examples in the Bible of angels appearing to man. A few Bible narratives for further examples are listed below:

- An angel appeared to the shepherds, Luke 2:8-14

- An angel set Peter free, Acts 12:5-11

- The angel Gabriel told Mary she would bring forth Jesus, the promised child, Luke 1:26-33

- An angel wrestled with Jacob, Genesis 32:24

- An angel appeared to the woman at Christ's tomb, Luke 24:1-10

18. AREN'T ANGELS FEMALES?

☐ No. Contrary to what we see in many pictures and greeting cards, God created the angels as males only. In the Old Testament they are called "sons of God." In the New Testament they are called "ministering spirits." They are sent forth today as ministering spirits to help Disciples in their times of need. Below are other related facts about angels:

- Angels are a spirit and can take on the form of man at will.

- "Yea, whiles I was speaking in prayer, even the man Gabriel, whom I had seen in the vision at the beginning, being caused to fly swiftly, touched me about the time of the evening oblation." Daniel 9:21

☐ The title, "Sons of God" has a different meaning in the Old Testament that it has in the New Testament.

☐ In the Old Testament, this term referred to the angels. A "son of God" denotes a being brought into form by a creative act of God. God created the angels and Adam (man). Adam was created in the likeness of God (Genesis 5:1; Luke 3:38); but, the descendants of Adam were born in his (mankind's) likeness.

> • Genesis 5:3 reads, " . . . Adam begat a son in his own likeness, after his image."

> • Thus we must understand that all the descendants of Adam were called "sons of men." It was not until the new birth experience that a person could become a "son of God!"

> • "When the morning stars sang together, and all the sons of God shouted for joy." Job 38:7

☐ "Sons of God", in the New Testament applies to those who became God's sons through the new birth experience. John 1:12 reads, "But as many as received him, to them gave he power to become the sons of God, even to them that believe on his name."

19. CAN ANGELS CHOOSE TO OBEY OR DISOBEY GOD?

☐ Yes. Just as God gave the first man and woman the freedom to obey or disobey him, he gave the same freedom to the angels. Lucifer was once an angel. He ultimately choose to disobey God.

> • "For thou (Lucifer) hast said in thine heart, I will ascend into heaven, I will exalt my throne above the stars of God: I will sit also upon the mount of the congregation, in the sides of the north: I will ascend above the heights of the clouds; I will be like the most High." Isaiah 14:13-14

20. IN WHAT OTHER WAYS DO ANGELS SERVE ON OUR BEHALF?

☐ Not only do angels minister to Disciples in times of need. They also rejoice over new Disciples that come to Christ. They are encamped all around the children of God to deliver them from any evil. (Can you imagine a being so large and powerful as an angel dancing and spinning around over a person repenting and coming to Christ?)

> • "Are they not all ministering spirits, sent forth to minister for them who shall be heirs of salvation?" Hebrews 1:14

> • "The angel of the Lord encamped round about them that fear him, and delivereth them." Psalms 34:7

> • "Likewise I say unto you, there is joy in the presence of the angels of God over one sinner that repenteth." Luke 15:10

Chapter 5
LUCIFER AND HIS GANG
(The Story of the Fallen Angels)

21. HOW DID IT BEGIN?

☐ To understand the story of the fallen angels we must go back to the beginning. The Word of God declares that in the beginning the heaven and the earth were created. God ordered them into existence by the word of His mouth. When God created the heaven and the earth they were in perfect and beautiful order.

- "In the beginning God created the heaven and the earth." Genesis 1:1

- "Let them praise the name of the Lord; for he commanded and they were created." Psalms 148:5

22. WHAT WAS LUCIFER'S RESPONSIBILITY IN HEAVEN?

☐ Lucifer was the anointed angel who led the other angels in their worship and praise to God. This was his assignment. God gave him perfect beauty and wisdom. He also equipped him to lead the angels in praise to God for he created him with instruments built into his body.

- "You [Lucifer] were the anointed cherub that covers with overshadowing (wings), and I set you so. You were upon the holy mountain of God; you walked up and down in the midst of the stones of fire (like the paved work of gleaning sapphire stone upon which the God of Israel walked on Mount Sinai)." Ezekiel 28:14

• "Thou sealest up the sum, full of wisdom, and perfect in beauty. Thou hast been in Eden the garden of God; every precious stone was thy covering, the sardius, topaz, and the diamond, the beryl, the onyx, and jasper, the sapphire, the emerald, and the carbuncle, and gold: the workmanship of thy tabrets and of thy pipes was prepared in thee in the day that thou was created." Ezekiel 28:12-13

23. DID LUCIFER REMAIN LOYAL TO GOD?

☐ No. Lucifer did not remain loyal to God; he coveted (desired for himself) the worship and adoration that belonged to God and attempted to take God's throne. Because of this great sin God cast him forth from heaven. God will not allow His glory to be given to another. How foolish of Lucifer even to think he could be equated with God (Jehovah Elyon, the Lord Most High).

• "For thou hast said in thine heart, I will ascend into heaven, I will exalt my throne above the stars of God: I will sit also upon the mount of the congregation in the sides of the north; I will ascend above the heights of the clouds; I will be like the most High." Isaiah 14:13-14

24. WAS LUCIFER THE ONLY ANGEL PUNISHED FOR THE SIN?

☐ No. Lucifer was not the only one NOT punished for the sin. Thousands of angels who followed Lucifer in his rebellion (disobedience) were cast forth from heaven with him.

• "I am the Lord: that is my name: and my glory will I not give to another, neither my praise to graven images." Isaiah 42:8

• "And he (Jesus) said unto them, I beheld Satan as lightning fall from heaven." Luke 10:18

• "And the great dragon was cast out, that old serpent, called the Devil, and Satan, which deceiveth the whole world: he was cast out into the earth, and his angels were cast out with him." Revelation 12:9

25. WHERE WERE LUCIFER AND HIS SINNING ANGELS CAST?

☐ Lucifer and the sinning angels were cast forth to inhabit the earth and its atmosphere.

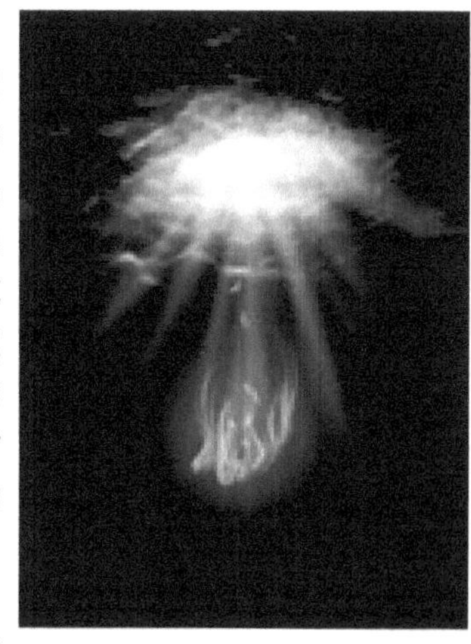

• "Be sober, be vigilant; because your adversary the devil, as a roaring lion, walketh about, seeking whom he may devour: Whom resist stedfast in the faith, knowing that the same afflictions are accomplished in your brethren that are in the world." 1 Peter 5:8-9

• "Put on the whole armour of God, that ye may be able to stand against the wiles of the devil. For we wrestle not against flesh and blood, but against principalities, against powers, against the rulers of the darkness of this world, against spiritual wickedness in high places." Ephesians 6:11-12

26. WHAT HAPPENED TO THE EARTH BECAUSE OF LUCIFER AND HIS FALLEN ANGELS BEING CAST FROM HEAVEN?

☐ When Lucifer was cast from heaven, the earth underwent a terrible upheaval. All things that were once created and were functioning orderly were disrupted and out of order. God's beautiful heaven and earth was without form and void.

• "Behold, the LORD maketh the earth empty, and maketh it waste, and turneth it upside down, and scattereth abroad the inhabitants thereof." Isaiah 24:1

• "And the earth was without form, and void; and darkness was upon the face of the deep. And the Spirit of God moved upon the face of the waters." Genesis 1:2

27. WHO IS SATAN? WHAT ARE DEMONS?

☐ The name Satan and Lucifer refer of the same person. After Lucifer was cast from Heaven, the scripture makes reference to him as "Satan." The angels who sinned with Lucifer are called demons. ("The Devil," is also a reference name for Satan.)

• "And the LORD said unto Satan, Whence comest thou? Then Satan answered the LORD, and said, From going to and fro in the earth, and from walking up and down in it." Job 1:7

• "And the great dragon was cast out, that old serpent, called the Devil, and Satan, which deceiveth the whole world: he was cast out into the earth, and his angels were cast out with him." Revelation 12:9

Chapter 6
RESTORING ORDER IN THE EARTH
(God said . . . "Let there be")

28. HOW DID GOD CAUSE THE EARTH TO COME BACK INTO ORDER AFTER LUCIFER'S REBELLION?

☐ God did this great task by simply speaking everything back into order and operation. His words are so powerful that it was done when he had commanded it!

- "And God said, Let there be a firmament in the midst of the waters, and let it divide the waters from the waters." Genesis 1:6

- "And God said, Let the waters under the heaven be gathered together unto one lace, and let the dry land appear: and it was so." Genesis 1:9

29. IN WHAT ORDER DID GOD DO ALL THIS RESTORATION?

☐ God restored order on earth by doing certain works of re-creation on certain days. Refer to Genesis 1:3 31, and Genesis 2:1 2, then look at the order of restored works:

- LIGHT. God divided the light from darkness, calling the darkness Night and the day (Cosmic) Light.

- FIRMAMENT. God separated the firmament(sky,heavens)anddivided the waters that were under the heaven from the waters that were above the heaven.

- DRY LAND. God made the water under the firmament (sky, heaven) gather together so dry land would appear and called forth grass, herb and fruit trees.

• SOLAR LIGHT & MOON. God caused the light to divide the day from the night within the firmament (sky). This was the solar light or sun. The moon and stars were also restored.

• FISH, FOWL & BIRDS. Moving creatures from the waters, fowl (birds) and all winged creatures were restored.

• CATTLE, BEASTS & MANKIND. Cattle, creeping things, and beasts of the earth were restored. Man was created.

• NOTHING - GOD RESTED ON THE 7TH DAY.

• "And God saw every thing that he had made, and, behold, it was very good. And the evening and the morning were the sixth day. Thus the heavens and the earth were finished, and all the host of them. And on the seventh day God ended his work which he had made; and he rested on the seventh day from all his work which he had made." Genesis 1:31,2:1 2

Chapter 7
MAN & WOMAN
(God's Special Creation)

30. HOW DID GOD CREATE THE MAN AND WOMAN?

☐ God created man from the dust of the ground and breathed life into his nostrils. God called him Adam. Later God created woman from a rib which he removed from Adam's side while Adam slept. God created man (Adam and Eve) in His own image.

> • "And God said, Let us make man in our image, after our likeness: and let them have dominion over the fish of the sea, and over the fowl of the air, and over the cattle, and over all the earth, and over every creeping thing that creepeth upon the earth. So God created man in his own image, in the image of God created he him; male and female created he them." Genesis 1:26-27

> • "And the LORD God formed man of the dust of the ground, and breathed into his nostrils the breath of life; and man became a living soul." Genesis 2:7

31. HOW ARE WE CREATED LIKE GOD?

☐ When the scriptures states that we were created in the image and likeness of God, it simply means that we had a similar spirit with the capacity to be aware of God. This knowing or awareness of God was given to us by the Almighty himself. Man was created also perfectly holy, righteous, and was given a free will to choose the ways of God or to deviate from them. Man even had the ability built in him by God to reproduce life. Let's take a look at the list of original man's resemblances to God:

• GOD CREATED MAN AND WOMAN - Man can reproduce life. The scripture in Genesis 1:27 29 tells man to multiply after his kind.

• GOD IS ETERNAL - Man, because of his three dimensions (spirit, soul, and body) particularly SPIRIT, will also live eternally.

• GOD HAS RULE OVER ALL THINGS - Man was told by God to have dominion over all things.

• GOD IS SPIRIT - Man has a greater capacity for spiritual things as well.

• GOD IS HOLY - Man was created perfectly holy as well.

• "But there is a spirit in man: and the inspiration of the Almighty giveth them understanding." Job 32:8

• "And God said, Let us make man in our image, after our likeness: and let them have dominion over the fish of the sea, and over the fowl of the air, and over the cattle, and over all the earth, and over every creeping thing that creepeth upon the earth. So God created man in his own image, in the image of God created he him; male and female created he them." Genesis 1:27-28

32. DO WE STILL BEAR THE IMAGE AND LIKENESS OF GOD?

☐ No. Man lost the image of God through the fall of Adam and Eve.

☐ This is how it happened. When God created man and the woman he placed them in a beautiful garden - Eden. Man had free access to every area of the garden and could eat of every fruit in the garden; however, God placed one restriction upon man. He was not to eat of the Tree of the Knowledge of Good and Evil. This was the only tree he was not to eat fruit from. Man had a free will and would have to choose to be obedient to God or satisfy his curiosity. He chose to satisfy his curiosity and ate of the forbidden tree. This was sin. Sin (disobedience) breaks our fellowship or relationship with God. Man's spirit died

from being attuned and aware of God and God had to sever mankind from the garden. Here, the image and likeness of God was lost.

☐ When a person receives Christ, restoration begins again. His spirit is born again. He begins to bear the heavenly image and His attributes. Complete restoration (full renewal of the image of God) will be reached when we get to heaven. Once receiving Christ, man is again made holy but his mind must be continuously renewed by the word of God to develop into being like Christ. The scripture declares that only in the resurrection that man will be restored into the image of God. At that time we shall be like Him.

> • "Beloved, now are we the sons of God, and it doth not yet appear what we shall be: but we know that, when he shall appear, we shall be like him; for we shall see him as he is." 1 John 3:2

Chapter 8
WHAT AM I MADE OF?
(The Dimensions of Man)

33. WHAT ARE THE DIMENSIONS OR COMPONENTS OF MAN?

☐ All mankind have three dimensions (parts) to their make up: SPIRIT, SOUL, and BODY.

- "For the word of God is quick, and powerful, and sharper than any two-edged sword, piercing even to the dividing asunder of soul and spirit, and of the joints and marrow, and is a discerner of the thoughts and intents of the heart." Hebrews 4:12

- "And the LORD God formed man of the dust of the ground, and breathed into his nostrils the breath of life; and man became a living soul." Genesis 2:7

- "But there is a spirit in man: and the inspiration of the Almighty giveth them understanding." Job 32:8

34. WHAT IS THE IMPORTANCE OF THE BODY?

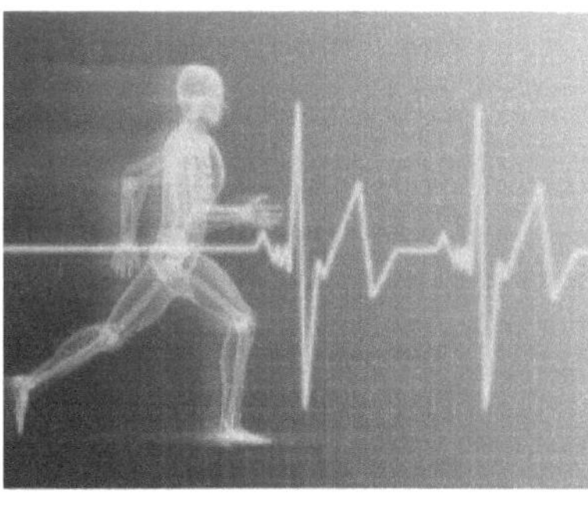

☐ The body is the part of man that deals or relate with the physical realm. Think of it as the house or outward shell of man. We are to keep our bodies holy (pure, clean) unto God. The body is to be brought into subjection (control) of our spirit. God doesn't want disciples ruled by their fleshly desires.

- "What? know ye not that your body is the temple of the Holy Ghost which is in you, which ye have of God, and ye are not your own? For ye are bought with a price: therefore glorify God in your body, and in your spirit, which are God's." 1 Corinthians 6:19-20

35. WHAT IS THE SOUL OF MAN?

☐ The soul is the part of man that deals with his mind (intellect), will (desire) and emotions (feelings). It's the mental dimension of man, the area of thinking, reasoning and expression. Just as disciples' bodies are to be presented to God as a holy sacrifice of service, there is a requirement also for man to renew his mind (change his thoughts and attitudes) to be pleasing to God. Reading the Word of God can only do this.

- "For the word of God is quick, and powerful, and sharper than any two-edged sword, piercing even to the dividing asunder of soul and spirit, and of the joints and marrow, and is a discerner of the thoughts and intents of the heart." Hebrews 4:12

36. WHAT IS THE SPIRIT OF MAN?

☐ The spirit (pneuma) is the dimension of man that deals with the spiritual insight and awareness of God. This is the God knowing part of man's being. God designed the spirit to rule and guide man's soul and body. It operates the faculties of faith, hope, reverence, prayer, praise and worship.

☐ In the Garden of Eden before man sinned, he was in a perfect spiritual state with God. When man fell through the sin of Adam, the spirit became dormant, asleep or deadened. The soul and body were left to rule man. This is the current state of an unregenerate man (not born again in Christ) today, either rule by the soul or physically ruled.

☐ Once a person receives Christ into his life chamber the spirit man is born again or awakened. Man again can receive impressions from God because his spirit is now awakened and attuned to hear what God is saying. God's Holy Spirit will communicate to our spirit the "deep things" of God for our life.

☐ Beliefs and concepts also enter the spirit through our mind. Whatever is pondered and meditated upon in our mind will eventually settle into our spirit. That's why it's vitally important to renew or feed our mind the word of God instead of errant thoughts and ideas. The mind will transfer to our spirit whatever is being fed into it. The spirit only grows through being fed the word of God.

Chapter 9
COVENANT
(God's Commitment With Mankind)

37. WHAT IS A COVENANT?

☐ In English, the word "covenant" means a mutual agreement or understanding between two or more parties; a contract; a binding commitment to do or not to do a certain thing.

☐ In the Hebrew language (Old Testament), the word means a compact made by passing between flesh and blood, which implies cutting; a treaty, an alliance, and an ordinance.

☐ In the Greek (New Testament), the word refers to a will or declaration, an arrangement, to place together or put together by mutual agreement.

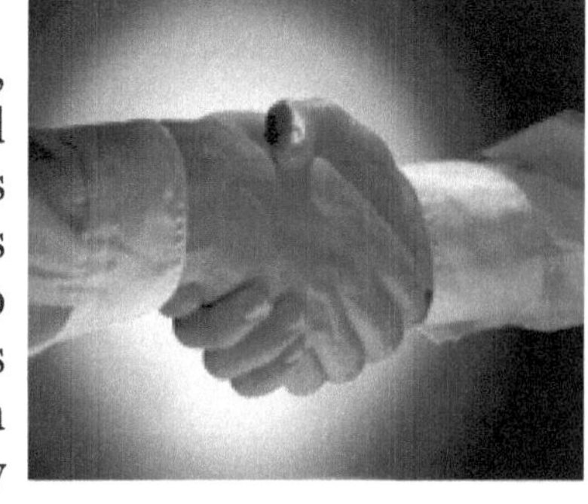

☐ With God, "cutting" a covenant, meant establishing an eternal mutual agreement of promises with man based upon man's obedience and submission to God's requirements. Covenants were initiated and sealed through the shedding of blood. Only the death of the reneging partner could also break the covenant. When God entered into covenant with mankind, he had no intentions of going back on his promises. He guaranteed his fulfilling of his promises by swearing by Himself.

> • "For when God made promise to Abraham, because he could swear by no greater, he sware by himself, Saying, Surely blessing I will bless thee, and multiplying I will multiply thee. And so, after he had patiently endured, he obtained the promise. For men verily swear by the greater: and an oath for confirmation is to them an end of all strife. Wherein God, willing more

abundantly to show unto the heirs of promise the immutability of his counsel, confirmed it by an oath: That by two immutable things, in which it was impossible for God to lie, we might have a strong consolation, who have fled for refuge to lay hold upon the hope set before us." Hebrews 6:13-18

38. WHERE DID COVENANTS ORIGINATE?

☐ Covenants originated from God. He made covenant with man. Through the promises and benefits of these covenants, God revealed his heart and love toward mankind. Covenants are the greatest manifestations and declarations of God's love and mercy toward man.

39. WITH WHOM DID GOD MAKE COVENANTS?

☐ God made covenants with ADAM & EVE, ABRAHAM, ISAAC, ISRAEL (JACOB), NOAH, MOSES, JOSHUA, DAVID, SOLOMON, and JESUS CHRIST.

40. WHY MAKE A COVENANT WITH ANOTHER PARTY?

☐ The strengths and weaknesses of the both parties are brought together for the benefit of both groups. Each party was to provide their best resources in behalf of the other party member's family. Failure to do so resulted in the death of the withholding party's family.

☐ Anyone who enters a covenant obligates himself to relationship with a partner. This obligation provided a strong sense of security - it was backed by the life of the covenant partner. When we are secure in our covenant with God, we are confident of his love and commitment toward us and we are free to be used and developed as vessels for His purpose and expression.

Chapter 10
ADAM & EVE'S COVENANT WITH GOD
(The Garden of Eden)

41. WHAT COVENANT DID GOD MAKE WITH ADAM & EVE?

☐ After God created man he made a garden called Eden where he placed man to live. His job was to enjoy his home and to cultivate it (cause it to grow and flourish). The scripture says that God would come down (to Eden) "in the cool of the day" to fellowship with Adam and Eve. Man had complete fellowship with God. There was no sin in the earth and man experienced no barriers between him and God. During this time in life man enjoyed spiritual and natural wholeness.

☐ This was the setting ... the Garden of Eden: Some area of the restored earth that was called back into order after the fall of Lucifer. It was a beautiful place, probably a true "wonder" of the world, watered naturally from mist rising up from the ground. Bird life filled the skies, the land; full of wildlife, rich with color and beautiful plant life, and pure rivers and streams flowed through the land. This was the paradise where God talked (fellowshipped) with man.

☐ Who were there? Adam and Eve, God's prized human creations. Here in Eden, man had knowledge of only good, not evil.

42. WHERE THERE DANGERS TO THIS BLISSFUL STATE IN THE GARDEN?

☐ Yes. God warned man of existing danger by telling him of the presence of the Tree of Knowledge of Good and Evil that was in the garden. The Tree of Life and all other trees in the garden were bearing fruit good for man to eat, but God commanded him not to eat of the Tree of Knowledge of Good and Evil. God created man with a free will; therefore, he was not a "robot" and thus free to obey or disobey the command of God. The two trees in the garden and God's command to man, "THOU SHALT NOT", were actually a test to see if man would obey the warning of God by an act of his own will.

• "And the LORD God commanded the man, saying, Of every tree of the garden thou mayest freely eat: But of the tree of the knowledge of good and evil, thou shalt not eat of it: for in the day that thou eatest thereof thou shalt surely die." Genesis 2:16-17

• "And out of the ground made the LORD God to grow every tree that is pleasant to the sight, and good for food; the tree of life also in the midst of the garden, and the tree of knowledge of good and evil." Genesis 2:9

43. WHAT WAS THE DIFFERENCE BETWEEN THESE TWO TREES?

☐ THE TREE OF LIFE was a representation of Christ. It represented the source of life, knowledge, love, wisdom and peace. The fruit of this tree held the power of everlasting life. The scripture also does not indicate that the fruit was an apple as some religious folks have described it. It was a "type" (a person or thing believed to foreshadow another person) of Christ and speaks of the individual who chooses Christ into their life. Had they eaten of this fruit it would not have been necessary for Christ to have come to the earth as a man and die on the cross. Eating of the Tree of Life for Adam and Eve represented dependence upon God.

• "And out of the ground made the LORD God to grow every tree that is pleasant to the sight, and good for food; the tree of life also in the midst of the garden, and the tree of knowledge of good and evil." Genesis 2:9

• "I am the living bread which came down from heaven: if any man eat of this bread, he shall live for ever: and the bread that I will give is my flesh, which I will give for the life of the world." John 6:51

• "In him was life; and the life was the light of men." John 1:4

• "In whom are hid all the treasures of wisdom and knowledge" Colossians 2:3

☐ THE TREE OF THE KNOWLEDGE OF GOOD AND EVIL was a representation of sin and dependence upon all or any sources other than God. This would include the dictates of one's own mind, lusts of the flesh, intellect without the guidance of the Holy Spirit, and all knowledge of evil, guilt and sin.

• "And the serpent said unto the woman, Ye shall not surely die: For God doth know that in the day ye eat thereof, then your eyes shall be opened, and ye shall be as gods, knowing good and evil." Genesis 3:4-5

• "And the LORD God commanded the man, saying, Of every tree of the garden thou mayest freely eat: But of the tree of the knowledge of good and evil, thou shalt not eat of it: for in the day that thou eatest thereof thou shalt surely die." Genesis 2:16-17

• "There is a way which seemeth right unto a man, but the end thereof are the ways of death." Proverbs 14:12

44. WHAT WAS ADAM'S AND EVE'S DECISION TOWARDS GOD'S COMMAND?

☐ They both ate of the forbidden fruit. Adam directly disobeyed God's command and did nothing to stop the serpent from deceiving Eve. Satan deceived Eve to make this decision by speaking to them through the serpent.

> • "Now the serpent was more subtle than any beast of the field which the LORD God had made. And he said unto the woman, Yea, hath God said, Ye shall not eat of every tree of the garden? And the woman said unto the serpent, We may eat of the fruit of the trees of the garden: But of the fruit of the tree which is in the midst of the garden, God hath said, Ye shall not eat of it, neither shall ye touch it, lest ye die. And the serpent said unto the woman, Ye shall not surely die: For God doth know that in the day ye eat thereof, then your eyes shall be opened, and ye shall be as gods, knowing good and evil. And when the woman saw that the tree was good for food, and that it was pleasant to the eyes, and a tree to be desired to make one wise, she took of the fruit thereof, and did eat, and gave also unto her husband with her; and he did eat." Genesis 3:1-6

45. WHAT WAS SATAN'S PURPOSE IN TEMPTING EVE?

☐ Satan's purpose was to destroy God's plan of creating mankind to rule and reign over the earth and its inhabitants. God had given man dominion over all that moved upon the earth. Satan was jealous of this authority because the earth had been his assigned place to rule. This was before he had sinned and caused 1/3 of the angelic host to sin with him. As partial punishment, he was expelled from heaven. After he was cast from heaven, Satan was to inhabit (live in) the earth and

its atmosphere, stripped of all authority. God gave man the command and authority to subdue and have dominion over the earth.

> • "And he said unto them, I beheld Satan as lightning fall from heaven." Luke 10:18

> • "How art thou fallen from heaven, O Lucifer, son of the morning! how art thou cut down to the ground, which didst weaken the nations! For thou hast said in thine heart, I will ascend into heaven, I will exalt my throne above the stars of God: I will sit also upon the mount of the congregation, in the sides of the north: I will ascend above the heights of the clouds; I will be like the most High. Yet thou shalt be brought down to hell, to the sides of the pit." Isaiah 14:12-15

> • "And God said, Let us make man in our image, after our likeness: and let them have dominion over the fish of the sea, and over the fowl of the air, and over the cattle, and over all the earth, and over every creeping thing that creepeth upon the earth. So God created man in his own image, in the image of God created he him; male and female created he them. And God blessed them, and God said unto them, Be fruitful, and multiply, and replenish the earth, and subdue it: and have dominion over the fish of the sea, and over the fowl of the air, and over every living thing that moveth upon the earth." Genesis 1:26-28

☐ Satan's plan was for man to disobey God (just as he had done) hoping God would therefore turn over the rulership of the earth into his control again. God is looking for obedience and has given his Spirit to those who obey his commands!

> • "And we are his witnesses of these things; and so is also the Holy Ghost, whom God hath given to them that obey him." Acts 5:32

46. WHY DID ADAM AND EVE CHOOSE TO DISOBEY GOD?

☐ Satan deceived them by leading them to believe that God was withholding from them all good. They had no concept of what evil could be. God never told them about this, to their curiosity this sounded enticing, and this led them further towards Satan's lie.

☐ He convinced them to believe that they could be like "gods" themselves. Strangely enough, they didn't realize that they already were gods due to being made of God's image. Satan convinced them that they could survive and be happy on their own (independent) without God.

☐ Eve believed what Satan told her. She planted seeds of unbelief and deception (trickery) into her heart. She persuaded Adam to violate the commandment given to him by God not to eat of that tree's fruit. They chose to believe in Satan rather than to believe and trust in what God had said. These two seeds produced and caused Adam and Eve to sin, and in this, the fall of all mankind after them.

• "But of the fruit of the tree which is in the midst of the garden, God hath said, Ye shall not eat of it, neither shall ye touch it, lest ye die. And the serpent said unto the woman, Ye shall not surely die: For God doth know that in the day ye eat thereof, then your eyes shall be opened, and ye shall be as gods, knowing good and evil." Genesis 3:4-5

☐ Satan currently uses devices to attack those three main areas in our lives today. They are:

- Lust of the Flesh
- Lust of the Eyes
- Pride of Life

• "And when the woman saw that the tree was good for food, and that it was pleasant to the eyes, and a tree to be desired to make one wise, she took of the fruit thereof, and did eat, and gave also unto her husband with her; and he did eat." Genesis 3:6

47. WHAT WERE THE RESULTS OF ADAM AND EVE'S SIN?

☐ As a result of sin, Adam and Eve experienced guilt, shame, their relationship with God was severed and they were removed from the Garden of Eden. Sin will always bring guilt and shame when one has been made aware of righteousness. Adam, who once talked with God in the garden, was now afraid of God because of his sin. Sin severs man's relationship with God because God cannot have fellowship with unrighteousness (sinners) and remain true to Himself. Adam and Eve were also driven out of the Garden of Eden. It was God's love that drove them out so they would not eat of the Tree of Life thereafter and be eternally damned in that sinful spiritual state. Their sin produced the following results:

☐ Guilt And Shame:

• "And he said, I heard thy voice in the garden, and I was afraid, because I was naked; and I hid myself." Genesis 3:10

• "And unto Adam he said, Because thou hast hearkened unto the voice of thy wife, and hast eaten of the tree, of which I commanded thee, saying, Thou shalt not eat of it: cursed is the ground for thy sake; in sorrow shalt thou eat of it all the days of thy life;

Thorns also and thistles shall it bring forth to thee; and thou shalt eat the herb of the field; In the sweat of thy face shalt thou eat bread, till thou return unto the ground; for out of it wast thou taken: for dust thou art, and unto dust shalt thou return." Genesis 3:17-19

☐ Relationship With God Severed:

• "If I regard iniquity in my heart, the Lord will not hear me." Psalms 66:18

☐ Adam And Eve Were Driven Out Of The Garden:

• "And the LORD God said, Behold, the man is become as one of us, to know good and evil: and now, lest he put forth his hand, and take also of the tree of life, and eat, and live for ever: Therefore the LORD God sent him forth from the garden of Eden, to till the ground from whence he was taken. So he drove out the man; and he placed at the east of the garden of Eden Cherubims, and a flaming sword which turned every way, to keep the way of the tree of life." Genesis 3:22-24

48. WHO WAS PUNISHED FOR THESE SINS?

☐ The serpent, as the tool Satan used, was cursed to crawl upon his belly all the days of his life.

☐ The woman was to be ruled by man and endure the pains and sorrows of childbirth.

☐ The man was to labor with his hands to earn a living (his food and dwelling up keep). He would die and return to the earth as dust.

☐ The earth would begin to produce thorns, briars, weeds and other types of vegetation that would make it difficult for man to make his living by working with the soil.

• "And the LORD God said unto the serpent, Because thou hast done this, thou art cursed above all cattle, and above every beast of the field; upon thy belly shalt thou go, and dust shalt thou eat all the days of thy life: And I will put enmity between thee and the woman, and between thy seed and her seed; it shall bruise thy head, and thou shalt bruise his heel. Unto the woman he said, I will greatly multiply thy sorrow and thy conception; in sorrow thou shalt bring forth children; and thy desire shall be to thy husband, and he shall rule over thee. And unto Adam he said, because thou hast hearkened unto the voice of thy wife, and hast eaten of the tree, of which I commanded thee, saying, Thou shalt not eat of it: cursed is the ground for thy sake; in sorrow shalt thou eat of it all the days of thy life; Thorns also and thistles shall it bring forth to thee; and thou shalt eat the herb of the field; In the sweat of thy face shalt thou eat bread, till thou return unto the ground; for out of it wast thou taken: for dust thou art, and unto dust shalt thou return." Genesis 3:14-19

49. DID GOD LEAVE MAN WITHOUT HOPE AFTER HE HAD SINNED?

☐ No. God made a covenant (promise) that he would send a redeemer for man. The terms of this covenant promise was given in Genesis 3:15 16: ... "it will bruise thy head (Jesus would come as the redeemer and defeat Satan), and thou shalt bruise his heel," in other words, Satan would be permitted to inflict the sufferings upon Jesus that would lead Him to Calvary for crucifixion.

☐ In this passage of scripture God also made "coats of skins" for both Adam and Eve. It's inferred and we conclude that a covenant of blood was established between God and man and his sins were covered until true redemption (Jesus) would be sent.

• "And I will put enmity between thee and the woman, and between thy seed and her seed; it shall bruise thy head, and thou shalt bruise his heel. Unto the woman he said, I will greatly multiply thy sorrow and thy conception; in sorrow thou shalt bring forth children; and thy desire shall be to thy husband, and he shall rule over thee." Genesis 3:15-16

• "Unto Adam also and to his wife did the LORD God make coats of skins, and clothed them." Genesis 3:21

☐ Jesus' coming would open again the way to eternal life for man. Man would have forgiveness for his sin through Christ. This is the great hope of salvation!

• "For God, who commanded the light to shine out of darkness, hath shined in our hearts, to give the light of the knowledge of the glory of God in the face of Jesus Christ." 2 Corinthians 4:6

• "To open their eyes, and to turn them from darkness to light, and from the power of Satan unto God, that they may receive forgiveness of sins, and inheritance among them which are sanctified by faith that is in me." Acts 26:18

Chapter 11
LED BY MAN'S CONSCIENCE
(God's Covenant With Noah)

50. WHAT HAPPENED TO MANKIND AFTER THE FALL OF ADAM & EVE?

☐ Descendants from Adam & Eve were guided by their own conscience. Conscience is the voice of your spirit. It's the part of man that is knowledgeable of good and evil. It can produce fear and guilt, but it cannot keep a person from doing wrong. Mankind will be led into many sinful directions when guided only by the dictates of his conscience. God was gracious enough to permit man the freedom to choose between good and evil. In making choices that were according to the knowledge he possessed, man would have to suffer their consequences. God also wanted man to realize that his knowledge alone could not make him righteous.

51. TO WHAT EXTENT OF EVIL DID MAN'S CONSCIENCE LEAD HIM?

☐ Man became so progressively wicked that he involved himself in sinful (sexual) relationships with the angels (sons of God). These relationships produced giants upon the earth.

• "And it came to pass, when men began to multiply on the face of the earth, and daughters were born unto them, That the sons of God saw the daughters of men that they were fair; and they took them wives of all which they chose. And the LORD said, My spirit shall not always strive with man, for that he also is flesh: yet his days shall be an hundred and twenty years.

47

> There were giants in the earth in those days; and also after that, when the sons of God came in unto the daughters of men, and they bare children to them, the same became mighty men which were of old, men of renown." Genesis 6:1-4

52. DID ALL MEN INDULGE IN THIS GROSS WICKEDNESS?

☐ No. There was one righteous man by the name of Noah who kept himself and his family undefiled. God saw their obedience and love for him. God devised a plan to destroy all of mankind in the earth and yet deliver Noah's family in the midst of this vast destruction.

> • "And God saw that the wickedness of man was great in the earth, and that every imagination of the thoughts of his heart was only evil continually. And it repented the LORD that he had made man on the earth, and it grieved him at his heart. And the LORD said, I will destroy man whom I have created from the face of the earth; both man, and beast, and the creeping thing, and the fowls of the air; for it repenteth me that I have made them. But Noah found grace in the eyes of the LORD." Genesis 6:5-8

53. WHAT WAS THE COVENANT PLAN GOD ESTABLISHED WITH NOAH AND HIS FAMILY?

☐ God instructed Noah to build an ark, which was a large 3 -story rectangular boat the size of a professional football field. This was to provide a means of escape for him, his family and pairs of the animal kingdom. For 120 years, Noah and his family constructed the ark and preached to all mankind that it was going to rain on the earth.

☐ Until the day of the floods, there was no rain upon the earth. Men laughed and mocked them for their warnings. God's plan was to send a flood of waters to cover the earth and destroy all flesh for 40 days and nights.

☐ When the waters subsided, God promised (covenant) Noah that he would not destroy the earth again with water. He placed the "rainbow" (bow) in the sky as a reminder and symbol of His covenant with Noah.

> • "And I will establish my covenant with you; neither shall all flesh be cut off any more by the waters of a flood; neither shall there any more be a flood to destroy the earth. And God said, This is the token of the covenant which I make between me and you and every living creature that is with you, for perpetual generations: I do set my bow in the cloud, and it shall be for a token of a covenant between me and the earth. And it shall come to pass, when I bring a cloud over the earth, that the bow shall be seen in the cloud: And I will remember my covenant, which is between me and you and every living creature of all flesh; and the waters shall no more become a flood to destroy all flesh. And the bow shall be in the cloud; and I will look upon it, that I may remember the everlasting covenant between God and every living creature of all flesh that is upon the earth." Genesis 9:11-16

54. WHAT HAPPENED TO THE GIANTS?

☐ Those born before the flood were destroyed with all flesh. The people of God in various battles killed giants born after the flood. David and Goliath in 1 Samuel 17 (sample bible narrative):

> • David fought the giant by the power of the Lord

> • He stated that he stood before Goliath in the name of the God of Israel who would give him the victory

> • God directed David's sling to inflict death to the giant

55. WHAT WAS THE PUNISHMENT FOR THESE SINNING ANGELS?

☐ God delivered them unto chains of darkness in the center of the earth to await the final judgment.

• "For if God spared not the angels that sinned, but cast them down to hell, and delivered them into chains of darkness, to be reserved unto judgment." 2 Peter 2:4

• "And the angels which kept not their first estate, but left their own habitation, he hath reserved in everlasting chains under darkness unto the judgment of the great day. Even as Sodom and Gomorrha, and the cities about them in like manner, giving themselves over to fornication, and going after strange flesh, are set forth for an example, suffering the vengeance of eternal fire." Jude 6-7

56. WHAT DID GOD DO FOR NOAH AND HIS FAMILY AFTER THE FLOOD?

☐ God gave his family certain laws to abide by and allowed him the authority to stress these laws with others.

57. WHAT WERE THESE LAWS?

☐ Noah and his sons were to multiply and replenish the earth

• "And you, be ye fruitful, and multiply; bring forth abundantly in the earth, and multiply therein." Genesis 9:7

☐ Mankind was not to eat the BLOOD of animals (Until this time man did not eat the flesh of animals, now he could)

• "Every moving thing that liveth shall be meat for you; even as the green herb have I given you all things.

But flesh with the life thereof, which is the blood thereof, shall ye not eat." Genesis 9:3-4

☐ Mankind was given the authority to judge lawbreakers

• "Whoso sheddeth man's blood, by man shall his blood be shed: for in the image of God made he man." Genesis 9:6

☐ God knew that man could not be obedient to Him without experiencing an inward change of heart. It was necessary for man to realize that he could not still govern himself by his inward conscience and laws. Man had to realize his need for a Savior who could only open the way to an inward change of heart.

58. HOW DID GOD SET UP THE GOVERNING STRUCTURE FOR MAN?

☐ The sons of Noah were to have certain responsibilities. Shem was given the authority to govern. Japheth was to flow (assist) Shem in government. Ham (Canaan) was to be servant to the two of them.

• "And Noah awoke from his wine, and knew what his younger son had done unto him. And he said, Cursed be Canaan; a servant of servants shall he be unto his brethren. And he said, Blessed be the LORD God of Shem; and Canaan shall be his servant. God shall enlarge Japheth, and he shall dwell in the tents of Shem; and Canaan shall be his servant." Genesis 9:24-27

59. HOW WAS THE GOVERNING STRUCTURE FINALLY DISRUPTED?

☐ A descendant of Ham (Canaan) by the name of Nimrod came into authority and became a great hunter before the Lord. Nimrod was a great organizer of the people and formed labor teams to build a city with a tower called "Babel." His strategy was to have man congregate in one area or cities and develop technological systems to support massive population concentrations instead of spreading throughout the land as God had commanded.

☐ Nimrod's purpose for the tall tower was to provide a way of access back into the heavens or to God. Due to the sinful hearts of mankind, the city became sinful and wicked. Particularly within this tower all manner of spiritual wickedness took place (fornication, adultery, abortion, homosexuality, demonic worship, angelic worship, witchcraft, astrology, stealing etc.).

☐ Man cannot approach God in righteousness by his own efforts that's why mankind needs a Savior.

> • "And they said one to another, Go to, let us make brick, and burn them thoroughly. And they had brick for stone, and slime had they for mortar. And they said, Go to, let us build us a city and a tower, whose top may reach unto heaven; and let us make us a name, lest we be scattered abroad upon the face of the whole earth." Genesis 11:3-4

60. WHAT WAS GOD'S RESPONSE TO MAN'S WICKEDNESS?

☐ God admired their ingenuity, but knew that this would lead to greater wickedness. In order to stop their progression, God caused a confusion of their speech. This is the origin for different languages in the earth. As a result of the confusion in languages, man began to migrate all over the earth as God had originally intended.

• "And the LORD came down to see the city and the tower, which the children of men builded. And the LORD said, Behold, the people is one, and they have all one language; and this they begin to do: and now nothing will be restrained from them, which they have imagined to do. Go to, let us go down, and there confound their language, that they may not understand one another's speech. So the LORD scattered them abroad from thence upon the face of all the earth: and they left off to build the city. Therefore is the name of it called Babel; because the LORD did there confound the language of all the earth: and from thence did the LORD scatter them abroad upon the face of all the earth." Genesis 11:5-9

54

Chapter 12
GOD ESTABLISHES A FAMILY
(Covenant With Abraham)

61. WHAT DID MANKIND DO AFTER BEING DISPERSED FROM BABEL?

☐ After the Babelites were dispersed, descendants of Noah became idolaters (people who served strange gods). There was no record in the scripture of any righteous persons living during this time. God chose one man's family to start again. Abram (renamed Abraham) was chosen by God to set the standard and be set apart from idolatry. God told Abraham to leave his country and family to go to a land that God would reveal.

62. HOW DID GOD CUT COVENANT WITH ABRAHAM?

☐ God had him to cut a heifer, she goat, and a ram into halves, and lay them against each other. The turtledove and a young pigeon were laid there also. God caused a deep sleep to fall on Abraham and he spoke to him. God then passed (walked) between those pieces and consumed them as a smoking furnace and a burning lamp (fire).

• "And it came to pass, that, when the sun went down, and it was dark, behold a smoking furnace, and a burning lamp that passed between those pieces. In the same day the LORD made a covenant with Abram, saying, Unto thy seed have I given this land, from the river of Egypt unto the great river, the river Euphrates." Genesis 15:7-18

63. WHAT DID GOD COVENANT TO PROVIDE FOR ABRAHAM?

☐ To make of him a great nation, many descendants
☐ To give him personal blessings he desired
☐ He would be honored by many with great reputation
☐ He would be a funnel that others would be blessed

☐ God would curse his enemies
☐ God would bless those who loved him
☐ All families of the earth would be blessed through him

> • "Now the LORD had said unto Abram, Get thee out of thy country, and from thy kindred, and from thy father's house, unto a land that I will show thee: And I will make of thee a great nation, and I will bless thee, and make thy name great; and thou shalt be a blessing: And I will bless them that bless thee, and curse him that curseth thee: and in thee shall all families of the earth be blessed." Genesis 12:1-3

64. WHAT WERE THE PERSONAL BLESSINGS THAT ABRAHAM DESIRED?

☐ Abraham desired that he and Sarah, his barren (unable to bear a child) wife, would have a natural child even in their old age.

> • "And he said unto Abram, Know of a surety that thy seed shall be a stranger in a land that is not theirs, and shall serve them; and they shall afflict them four hundred years; And also that nation, whom they shall serve, will I judge: and afterward shall they come out with great substance. And thou shalt go to thy fathers in peace; thou shalt be buried in a good old age." Genesis 15:13-14

> • "He hath remembered his covenant for ever, the word which he commanded to a thousand generations. Which covenant he made with Abraham, and his oath unto Isaac; And confirmed the same unto Jacob for a law, and to Israel for an everlasting covenant: Saying, Unto thee will I give the land of Canaan, the lot of your inheritance." Psalms 105:8-11

65. DID GOD FULFILL HIS COVENANT TO ABRAHAM?

☐ Yes. God always fulfills his promises. Abraham and Sarah

did have their son Isaac, 25 years later (Abraham; age 99, Sarah at 89). The seed of Abraham grew into a large nation. God later used one of Abraham's great grandsons, Joseph, to be sent as a slave and then become prime minister in Egypt. Through this God caused Abraham's family to be preserved and prosperous during a world famine.

☐ They became so blessed as a nation that the Egyptian rulers became jealous and began to enslave the Israelites and dominate them. (See Genesis 26:17; Genesis 31,32; Genesis 37:41; and Exodus 2-7)

☐ Just as God fulfilled all he promised Abraham, he also will complete all he says to us. We must be like Abraham and not stumble at the promises of God, being fully persuaded that He will fulfill what He says!

> • "He staggered not at the promise of God through unbelief; but was strong in faith, giving glory to God; And being fully persuaded that, what he had promised, he was able also to perform. And therefore it was imputed to him for righteousness. Now it was not written for his sake alone, that it was imputed to him; But for us also, to whom it shall be imputed, if we believe on him that raised up Jesus our Lord from the dead; Who was delivered for our offences, and was raised again for our justification." Romans 4:20-25

66. HOW LONG WAS ISRAEL ENSLAVED TO THE EGYPTIANS?

☐ They were kept in bondage for 400 years until God rose up a deliver by the name of Moses in their fourth generation as a people.

> • "And he said unto Abram, Know of a surety that thy seed shall be a stranger in a land that is not theirs, and shall serve them; and they shall afflict them four hundred years; And also that nation, whom they shall serve, will I judge: and afterward shall they come out with great substance. And thou shalt go to thy fathers

in peace; thou shalt be buried in a good old age. But in the fourth generation they shall come hither again: for the iniquity of the Amorites is not yet full." Genesis 15:13-16

• "Thou shalt not bow down thyself to them, nor serve them: for I the LORD thy God am a jealous God, visiting the iniquity of the fathers upon the children unto the third and fourth generation of them that hate me." Exodus 20:5

67. WHAT WAS THE COVENANT GOD MADE WITH MOSES?

☐ The Mosaic Covenant was made with Israel after their exodus from Egypt at Mt. Sinai. The Law or Ten Commandments were introduced by God through Moses to serve as a "schoolmaster" to bring or point Israel to the need of a Savior, Christ Jesus.

68. WHAT WAS THE LAW?

☐ The Law was a set of Ten Commandments given to Israel through His servant Moses. These laws were to instruct man in the way he should live until the coming of Christ who would usher in an entirely different method for receiving righteousness. God wrote these Laws into man's heart. He also wanted to make them visible (able to be seen on tablets) for the people and speak to them. The Law was also given to make God's people a special nation set apart and different from all others.

• "Wherefore the law was our schoolmaster to bring us unto Christ, that we might be justified by faith." Galatians 3:24

• "For when the Gentiles, which have not the law, do by nature the things contained in the law, these, having not the law, are a law unto themselves: Which show the work of the law written in their hearts, their conscience also bearing witness, and their thoughts the mean while accusing or else excusing one another." Romans 2:14-15

• "Now therefore, if ye will obey my voice indeed, and keep my covenant, then ye shall be a peculiar treasure unto me above all people: for all the earth is mine." Exodus 19:5

Chapter 13
THE TEN COMMANDMENTS

69. WHAT IS THE FIRST COMMANDMENT?

• "Thou shalt have no other gods before me." Exodus 20:3

70. HOW DO I OBEY THE 1st COMMANDMENT?

☐ By serving the ONE and ONLY true and living God

• "...Then saith Jesus unto him, Get thee hence, Satan: for it is written, Thou shalt worship the Lord thy God, and him only shalt thou serve." Matthew 4:10

☐ By believing in the Trinity of God [God the Father, God the Son and God the Holy Spirit]

• "That all men should honour the Son, even as they honour the Father. He that honoureth not the Son honoureth not the Father which hath sent him." John 5:23

☐ By refusing to love, desire worship, or esteem as "God" any person or object. This includes friends, family favorite items, etc.

• "I am the LORD: that is my name: and my glory will I not give to another, neither my praise to graven images." Isaiah 42:8

71. WHAT IS THE SECOND COMMANDMENT?

• "Thou shalt not make unto thee any graven image." Exodus 20:4

72. HOW DO I OBEY THE 2nd COMMANDMENT?

☐ We should not bow, serve or make ourselves submissive to anything other than God. Idols are objects, figures or things, where we value or desire them more than we desire God. We ascribe unto them power and divine authority to rule and control us. They can be made of gold, silver, stone, and other corruptible substances. Figure features can be similar to those of birds, beasts, creeping things, mankind and/or combinations of the above. Worship of idols, called "graven images," is a sin that provokes God's jealous anger.

• "I am the LORD: that is my name: and my glory will I not give to another, neither my praise to graven images." Isaiah 42:8

• "Professing themselves to be wise, they became fools, And changed the glory of the uncorruptible God into an image made like to corruptible man, and to birds, and fourfooted beasts, and creeping things." Romans 1:22-23

• "Forasmuch then as we are the offspring of God, we ought not to think that the Godhead is like unto gold, or silver, or stone, graven by art and man's device." Acts 17:29

73. WHAT IS THE THIRD COMMANDMENT?

• "Thou shalt not take the name of the Lord thy God in vain." Exodus 20:7

74. HOW DO I OBEY THE 3rd COMMANDMENT?

☐ By always speaking honorably and reverently of God in all conversations.

☐ When required by legal authority to take an oath [a vow

to provide truthful legal testimony as a witness to something seen or heard], to always be truthful regardless of the consequences.

☐ Being committed to fulfilling any vows [promises and declarations made in God's presence such as ordination of ministers, marriage, dedication of children, etc.] made before God.

> • "And ye shall not swear by my name falsely, neither shalt thou profane the name of thy God: I am the LORD." Leviticus 19:12

> • "But above all things, my brethren, swear not, neither by heaven, neither by the earth, neither by any other oath: but let your yea be yea; and your nay, nay; lest ye fall into condemnation." James 5:12

75. WHAT IS THE FOURTH COMMANDMENT?

> • "Remember the sabbath day, to keep it holy." Exodus 29:8

76. HOW DO I OBEY THE 4th COMMANDMENT?

☐ The word "sabbath" in Hebrew means "rest." According to the law, on the seventh day man was to cease from all physical work or labor. God intended for man to rest and do only holy deeds unto Him on this day. When Jesus came, the scriptures state the He fulfilled the sabbath law by agreeing to submit Himself to the plan and purposes of God the Father and resting in His Will.

☐ When we accept Jesus, we must realize that ceasing from physical labor and doing good deeds alone can't make us acceptable to God. We keep this commandment by accepting Christ as Lord and His work of redemption through identification with His death, burial and resurrection. Resting in Christ is fulfilling the Sabbath. Our Sabbath is a life experience with Christ and not observance of a specific day. We rest in His work in us daily!

77. HOW IS IT THAT MOST BELIEVERS HAVE CHURCH SERVICES ON SUNDAYS?

☐ Most believers have come together to worship on Sundays because of convenience. Most businesses respect this day as such and are closed. Notice also that the apostles came together on the first day to break bread. They also had no regard for the sabbath "day" because they knew the Jesus of the sabbath.

• "Upon the first day of the week let every one of you lay by him in store, as God hath prospered him, that there be no gatherings when I come." 1 Corinthians 16:2

78. WHAT IS THE FIFTH COMMANDMENT?

• "Honour thy father and thy mother: that thy days may be long upon the land which the LORD thy God giveth thee." Exodus 20:12

79. HOW DO WE OBEY THE 5th COMMANDMENT?

☐ By loving, serving, showing kindness, and respecting our parents. We are to consider our parents as ambassadors of God. Honoring our parents will cause God to grant us long life.

☐ Obeying all people whom God has placed in authority over us. This includes authorities of law. Refusing to submit ourselves to authority placed over us is refusing to submit to God. He places people in authority over us. All this is done for our welfare and protection.

• "Honour thy father and mother; which is the first

commandment with promise; That it may be well with thee, and thou mayest live long on the earth." Ephesians 6:2-3

• "Submit yourselves to every ordinance of man for the Lord's sake: whether it be to the king, as supreme; Or unto governors, as unto them that are sent by him for the punishment of evildoers, and for the praise of them that do well. For so is the will of God, that with well doing ye may put to silence the ignorance of foolish men." 1 Peter 2:13-15

80. TO WHAT EXTENT DO WE OBEY AUTHORITY?

☐ We obey all authority unless the person in authority requires of us something sinful, which would violate the Word of God or require the denial of God Himself. The three [3] Hebrew men and Daniel refused to obey the sinful requests of the government officials in Daniel chapters 3-6.

81. WHAT IS THE SIXTH COMMANDMENT?

• "Thou shalt not kill." Exodus 20:13

82. HOW DO WE KEEP THIS COMMANDMENT?

☐ By being kind to our neighbors, family, and friends; NOT injuring them by physical abuse [fighting] or verbal abuse [destroying a person's self worth through words]. This obviously includes physically murdering someone. We have NO right to take a life without just punishment being executed upon us. The death penalty for certain crimes is right according to the scriptures.

• "For he is the minister of God to thee for good. But if thou do that which is evil, be afraid; for he beareth not the sword in vain: for he is the minister of God, a revenger to execute wrath upon him that doeth evil." Romans 13:4

> • "Whoso sheddeth man's blood, by man shall his blood be shed: for in the image of God made he man." Genesis 9:6

☐ By loving our neighbors and brothers in the Lord as well. Hatred is the root of murder.

> • "And be ye kind one to another, tenderhearted, forgiving one another, even as God for Christ's sake hath forgiven you." Ephesians 4:32

83. WHAT IS THE SEVENTH COMMANDMENT?

> • "Thou shalt not commit adultery." Exodus 20:14

84. WHAT IS ADULTERY?

☐ Adultery is having sexual relations with a person other than the marriage partner to whom vows (a covenant) are made. Physical contact or involvement in personal areas of bodies (even without actual sexual penetration) is considered adultery. This commandment also empathizes that the "source" and correction for adultery must come from the heart of man. Man conceives the idea first in his heart before he carries out the actual act.

> • "So ought men to love their wives as their own bodies. He that loveth his wife loveth himself." Matthew 5:28

> • "For out of the heart proceed evil thoughts, murders, adulteries, fornications, thefts, false witness, blasphemies." Matthew 15:19

85. WHAT IS REQUIRED IN THIS COMMANDMENT?

☐ God requires modest dress, pure words, and a Christ like example from his people. He requires us to saturate (fill) and renew our minds with his Word so that we will not hide sin in our hearts.

• "What? know ye not that your body is the temple of the Holy Ghost which is in you, which ye have of God, and ye are not your own? For ye are bought with a price: therefore glorify God in your body, and in your spirit, which are God's." 1 Corinthians 6:19-20

☐ God requires those who aren't married to lead chaste and holy lives. ALL sexual involvements are forbidden. Fornication is any sexual activities committed outside the marriage union. Therefore petting, sexual foreplay, caressing, masturbation, etc., should not be named among God's people. All sin originates in the heart of man. When sin is conceived in the heart it eventually brings forth death.

• "But fornication, and all uncleanness, or covetousness, let it not be once named among you, as becometh saints; Neither filthiness, nor foolish talking, nor jesting, which are not convenient: but rather giving of thanks." Ephesians 5:3-4

86. HOW MAY I AVOID FALLING FOR THE SIN OF FORNICATION?

☐ By repenting for meditating on these types of thoughts.

☐ Filling your mind with God's Word.

• "Finally, brethren, whatsoever things are true, whatsoever things are honest, whatsoever things are just, whatsoever things are pure, whatsoever things are lovely, whatsoever things are of good report; if there be any virtue, and if there be any praise, think on these things." Philippians 4:8

☐ Avoiding (run from) non christian settings, conversations, books, movies, games, etc. These lead to temptation and lust.

• "My son, if sinners entice thee, consent thou not." Proverbs 1:10

> • "Flee fornication. Every sin that a man doeth is without the body; but he that committeth fornication sinneth against his own body." 1 Corinthians 6:18

> • "Flee also youthful lusts: but follow righteousness, faith, charity, peace, with them that call on the Lord out of a pure heart." 2 Timothy 2:22

87. WHAT IS THE EIGHTH COMMANDMENT?

> • "Thou shalt not steal." Exodus 20:15

88. HOW DO WE KEEP THE EIGHTH COMMANDMENT?

☐ We keep this commandment by giving help to our neighbors whenever necessary. We should respect their personal property, and never damage or cheat them in any way. The Bible also states that taking part or partnership in stealing is sin. Buying stolen property is forbidden. We are all required to work with our hands for our necessities.

> • "Let him that stole steal no more: but rather let him labour, working with his hands the thing which is good, that he may have to give to him that needeth." Ephesians 4:28

> • "Whoso is partner with a thief hateth his own soul: he heareth cursing, and betrayeth it not." Proverbs 29:24

89. WHAT IS THE NINTH COMMANDMENT?

> • "Thou shalt not bear false witness against thy neighbor." Exodus 20:16

90. HOW DO WE KEEP THE NINTH COMMANDMENT?

☐ By being truthful in all things.

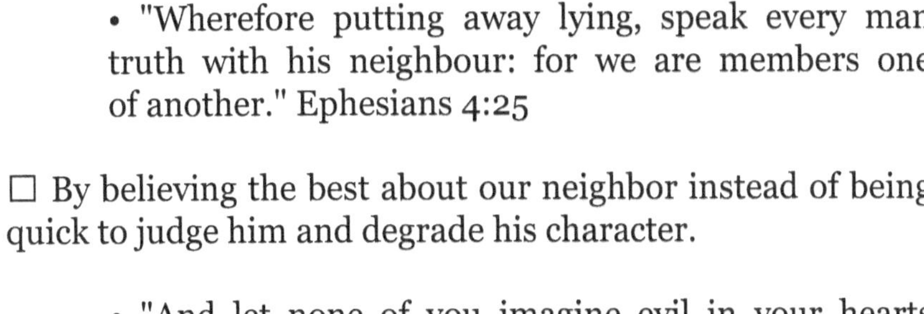

- "Wherefore putting away lying, speak every man truth with his neighbour: for we are members one of another." Ephesians 4:25

☐ By believing the best about our neighbor instead of being quick to judge him and degrade his character.

- "And let none of you imagine evil in your hearts against his neighbour; and love no false oath: for all these are things that I hate, saith the LORD." Zechariah 8:17

☐ By not spreading gossip about our neighbor or brother in the Lord. We also should not be revealing secrets about an individual that should remain concealed.

- "A talebearer revealeth secrets: but he that is of a faithful spirit concealeth the matter." Proverbs 11:13

☐ By being truthful while under oath in a legal setting (court).

- "A false witness shall not be unpunished, and he that speaketh lies shall not escape." Proverbs 19:5

☐ By truly loving our neighbor, this will cover his shortcomings.

- "And above all things have fervent charity among yourselves: for charity shall cover the multitude of sins." 1 Peter 4:8

91. WHAT IS THE TENTH COMMANDMENT?

- "Thou shalt not covet thy neighbour's house, thou shalt not covet thy neighbour's wife, nor his manservant, nor his maidservant, nor his ox, nor his ass, nor any thing that is thy neighbour's." Exodus 20:17

92. WHAT DOES IT MEAN TO "COVET"?

☐ To covet is to want something or someone that doesn't belong to you. This want is so strong that within the heart of the person he feels envy, jealousy, and selfishness.

> • "For this ye know, that no whoremonger, nor unclean person, nor covetous man, who is an idolater, hath any inheritance in the kingdom of Christ and of God." Ephesians 5:5

93. HOW DO WE OBEY THIS COMMANDMENT?

☐ By being content in what God has provided for us knowing that he will meet all our needs even as he meets those of our brother. We also must realize that God will make room for us in his body to do what he has called us to do as individuals. If we fail to realize this, covetousness in the church can be an enormous problem. Obeying this command in total will give the believer a resting peace in God's provision.

> • "And having food and raiment let us be therewith content. But they that will be rich fall into temptation and a snare, and into many foolish and hurtful lusts, which drown men in destruction and perdition. For the love of money is the root of all evil: which while some coveted after, they have erred from the faith, and pierced themselves through with many sorrows." 1 Timothy 6:8-10

> • "But seek ye first the kingdom of God, and his righteousness; and all these things shall be added unto you." Matthew 6:33

94. WHAT WAS GOD TRYING TO SHOW MANKIND IN REVEALING THESE COMMANDMENTS?

☐ God wanted us to see our attitude in life should be to

"love". Our love should be directed to God first and then toward all fellowmen. Yet man became increasingly evil, refused to submit and rejected God's statues.

95. WHAT HAPPENED TO ISRAEL AFTER THEY WERE GIVEN THE LAW?

☐ They became increasingly more evil and rejected God's Laws. God initially protected them from their enemies but they began to worship Baal and other strange idols and His Glory left them. They became enslaved by those nations around them.

☐ God did not forget His covenant with Abraham that He would send a deliverer for mankind. When God did send the "promised seed" [Jesus Christ] Israel was so evil and full of unbelief that said to the Roman rulers, "... let him be crucified and his blood be on us and our children ..." Many did not recognize Christ as the Messiah.

> • "And they rejected his statutes, and his covenant that he made with their fathers, and his testimonies which he testified against them; and they followed vanity, and became vain, and went after the heathen that were round about them, concerning whom the LORD had charged them, that they should not do like them. And they left all the commandments of the LORD their God, and made them molten images, even two calves, and made a grove, and worshipped all the host of heaven, and served Baal. And they caused their sons and their daughters to pass through the fire, and used divination and enchantments, and sold themselves to do evil in the sight of the LORD, to provoke him to anger." 2 Kings 17:15-17

Chapter 14
GOD SENDING THE MESSIAH
(The Birth of Jesus)

96. WHY DID GOD SEND HIS MESSIAH TO THE WORLD WHEN THEY DIDN'T WANT ONE?

☐ God remembered His Covenant with Abraham. He loved mankind so much that He sent His Son Jesus to the earth to give His life on the cross to redeem man and to establish His Church. Mankind would no longer be judged by Laws that he could not meet but on the basis of his acceptance or rejection of Christ. God is showing His favor and longsuffering toward mankind

97. WHERE WAS JESUS BORN?

☐ Jesus was born in the "city of David" in a town called Bethlehem of the province of Judea.

    • "And Joseph also went up from Galilee, out of the city of Nazareth, into Judaea, unto the city of David, which is called Bethlehem; (because he was of the house and lineage of David)." Luke 2:4

98. WHAT IS MEANT BY "JESUS THE GOD-MAN"?

☐ This phrase means that Jesus, although born of a natural woman, did not have an earthly father. The Holy Ghost conceived Jesus' flesh and overshadowed Mary so that he could be born both man and deity [of God]. Jesus allowed Himself to be born through flesh in a woman so that He could take on the likeness of mankind.

    • "And the angel answered and said unto her, The Holy Ghost shall come upon thee, and the power of the Highest shall overshadow thee: therefore also that holy thing which shall be born of thee shall be called the Son of God." Luke 1:35

• "Now the birth of Jesus Christ was on this wise: When as his mother Mary was espoused to Joseph, before they came together, she was found with child of the Holy Ghost." Matthew 1:18-25

99. HOW WAS JESUS TRUE GOD IN THE FLESH?

☐ Jesus was truly ONE with God from the beginning. The scriptures refer to Him being in the beginning with God and a part of the re creative work of God. The scriptures also refer to Jesus being the same spirit who took on flesh and dwelt with mankind.

• "In the beginning was the Word, and the Word was with God, and the Word was God. The same was in the beginning with God. All things were made by him; and without him was not any thing made that was made." John 1:1-3

• "For in him dwelleth all the fulness of the Godhead bodily." Colossians 2:9

• "Who being the brightness of his glory, and the express image of his person, and upholding all things by the word of his power, when he had by himself purged our sins, sat down on the right hand of the Majesty on high." Hebrews 1:3

100. HOW DID JESUS EXPRESS HIMSELF AS TRUE MAN?

☐ He became of flesh and blood at the time of his conception and placement into the womb of Mary. This is called the incarnation.

• "For unto us a child is born, unto us a son is given: and the government shall be upon his shoulder: and his name shall be called Wonderful, Counselor, The mighty God, The everlasting Father, The Prince of Peace." Isaiah 9:6

☐ We must remember that when Jesus was on the earth he ate, slept, wept, and experienced all that we do [except practicing sin] that he might be able to identify with us.

☐ At the finished work of Calvary he bore the weight and penalty for all sin for mankind as a man. He then became our mediator before God the Father.

• "For there is one God, and one mediator between God and men, the man Christ Jesus." 1 Timothy 2:5

101. WHAT WAS THE TRUE IDENTITY OF JESUS THE GOD MAN?

☐ According to the angel sent by God, Jesus was to be called the "Son of God". The scriptures repeatedly let us know that God sent His only Son by a woman to dwell with mankind.

• "And the Word was made flesh, and dwelt among us, (and we beheld his glory, the glory as of the only begotten of the Father,) full of grace and truth." John 1:14

102. HOW DOES THIS RELATE TO SALVATION FOR ME?

☐ The first step to salvation is to believe that Jesus Christ was not just a man, but that He IS the incarnate God Man CHRIST. He was born of the seed of the Holy Ghost. He had no natural father. The Holy Ghost placed him into the womb of Mary. He was sent by God to restore mankind back to fellowship with God, since Adam's sin had separated us from God in the beginning. The restoration of this fellowship became salvation for mankind. Mankind now has the opportunity to live in peace with his God eternally.

• "Now the birth of Jesus Christ was on this wise: When as his mother Mary was espoused to Joseph, before they came together, she was found with child of the Holy Ghost. Then Joseph her husband, being a just man, and not willing to make her a public example, was minded to put her away privily. But while he thought on these things, behold, the angel of the Lord appeared unto him in a dream, saying, Joseph, thou son of David, fear not to take unto thee Mary thy wife: for that which is conceived in her is of the Holy Ghost. And she shall bring forth a son, and thou shalt call his name JESUS: for he shall save his people from their sins. Now all this was done, that it might be fulfilled which was spoken of the Lord by the prophet, saying, behold, a virgin shall be with child, and shall bring forth a son, and they shall call his name Emmanuel, which being interpreted is, God with us. Then Joseph being raised from sleep did as the angel of the Lord had bidden him, and took unto him his wife: And knew her not till she had brought forth her firstborn son: and he called his name JESUS." Matthew 1:18-25

• "My little children, these things write I unto you, that ye sin not. And if any man sin, we have an advocate with the Father, Jesus Christ the righteous: And he is the propitiation for our sins: and not for ours only, but also for the sins of the whole world." 1 John 2:1 2

Chapter 15
KEYS TO REDEMPTION
(What Must I Believe?)

103. WHAT MUST I BELIEVE IN ORDER TO BE RESTORED INTO FELLOWSHIP WITH GOD?

☐ In order to receive Christ and be restored into fellowship with the Father you must believe in: the Incarnation; the Redemption; the Resurrection; and the Ascension of Christ.

104. WHAT DOES IT MEAN TO BELIEVE IN THE REDEMPTION?

☐ Believing in the Redemption is to believe that Jesus Christ died as the redeemer of all mankind. It's also to believe that His life and death were sufficient ransom to open again the way of eternal happiness and peace for mankind.

• "Who his own self bare our sins in his own body on the tree that we, being dead to sins, should live unto righteousness: by whose stripes ye were healed." 1 Peter 2:24

• "For God so loved the world, that he gave his only begotten Son, that whosoever believeth in him should not perish, but have everlasting life. For God sent not his Son into the world to condemn the world; but that the world through him might be saved." John 3:16-17

105. WHAT ARE SOME OF THE FACT OF THE REDEMPTION TRUTH?

☐ It was for our sakes that He came into this world and gave of Himself for our benefit.

> • "For ye know the grace of our Lord Jesus Christ, that, though he was rich, yet for your sakes he became poor, that ye through his poverty might be rich." 2 Corinthians 8:9

☐ Though he was the Christ, men received him not, but despised and rejected him.

> • "He is despised and rejected of men; a man of sorrows, and acquainted with grief: and we hid as it were our faces from him; he was despised, and we esteemed him not." Isaiah 53:3

☐ Pontius Pilate, the governor, scourged [beat] Jesus and under his jurisdiction Jesus suffered tremendously, even to the point of death on a cross.

> • "Then Pilate therefore took Jesus, and scourged him. And the soldiers platted a crown of thorns, and put it on his head, and they put on him a purple robe, And said, Hail, King of the Jews! and they smote him with their hands." John 19:1-3

> • "Then delivered he him therefore unto them to be crucified. And they took Jesus, and led him away. And he bearing his cross went forth into a place called the place of a skull, which is called in the Hebrew Golgotha: Where they crucified him, and two others with him, on either side one, and Jesus in the midst." John 19:16-18

☐ Christ paid our penalty for sin with his own blood. We were the ones condemned to death, but he bore our sins. Because of the shedding of his blood, we who believe in this redemptive work of Christ are free from the slavery of sin and the sting of death. Death for the believer is to be in the presence of God!

• "O death, where is thy sting? O grave, where is thy victory? The sting of death is sin; and the strength of sin is the law. But thanks be to God, which giveth us the victory through our Lord Jesus Christ." 1 Corinthians 15:55-57

•"Forasmuch as ye know that ye were not redeemed with corruptible things, as silver and gold, from your vain conversation received by tradition from your fathers; But with the precious blood of Christ, as of a lamb without blemish and without spot." 1 Peter 1:18-19

☐ Believing on his death by the cross and the shedding of the blood of Jesus Christ for sins is a message for all mankind. Christ came for all who will believe in him as The Redeemer!

• "For the Son of man is come to save that which was lost." Matthew 18:11

• "But if we walk in the light, as he is in the light, we have fellowship one with another, and the blood of Jesus Christ his Son cleanseth us from all sin." 1 John 1:7

• "And he is the propitiation for our sins: and not for ours only, but also for the sins of the whole world." 1 John 2:2

106. WHAT ARE SOME OF THE FACTS OF THE RESURRECTION TRUTH?

☐ After the crucifixion [death] of Christ, he remained in the grave three [3] days. After the 3 days, he arose from the dead.

• "Him God raised up the third day, and showed him openly; Not to all the people, but unto witnesses chosen before of God, even to us, who did eat and drink with him after he rose from the dead." Acts 10:40-41

☐ During the three days Christ's body was in the grave his spirit and soul went down to "sheol" [temporary abode for the dead]. He went there to release the righteous men and women who were living before Christ came on the earth. This had to be done because these righteous souls were in a comfortable and peaceful compartment in sheol, isolated from the access of wicked persons, awaiting the completion of the redemptive plan for them to be escorted to be with God in paradise. He also went to show himself to sinning angels and all who fell with Lucifer [Satan] proving that he is the Christ who was promised to come and destroy [bruise] the head of the Devil. Satan, through the crucifixion, sought to destroy Christ and thereby stop God's redemptive plan. Christ spoiled his plan completely and is alive forevermore!

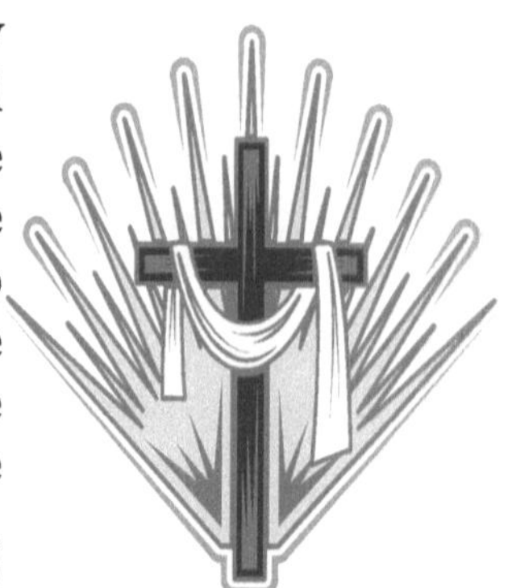

• "Wherefore he saith, When he ascended up on high, he led captivity captive, and gave gifts unto men. (Now that he ascended, what is it but that he also descended first into the lower parts of the earth? He that descended is the same also that ascended up far above all heavens, that he might fill all things.)" Ephesians 4:8-10

• "And I will put enmity between thee and the woman, and between thy seed and her seed; it shall bruise thy head, and thou shalt bruise his heel." Genesis 3:15

• "Because thou wilt not leave my soul in hell, neither wilt thou suffer thine Holy One to see corruption." Acts 2:27

☐ Christ appeared after his ascension to many on earth in a glorified [incorruptible] body. By this his disciples knew with confirmation that surely HE IS the CHRIST because they witnessed his death three days before. By the resurrection, the disciples, and even unbelievers were converted to believe, came to know that the doctrine of Christ is true.

• "To whom also he showed himself alive after his passion by many infallible proofs, being seen of them forty days, and speaking of the things pertaining to the kingdom of God." Acts 1:3

• "Jesus saith unto her, Touch me not; for I am not yet ascended to my Father: but go to my brethren, and say unto them, I ascend unto my Father, and your Father; and to my God, and your God." John 20:17

• "And if Christ be not raised, your faith is vain; ye are yet in your sins." 1 Corinthians 15:17

107. WHAT ARE SOME OF THE FACTS OF THE ASCENSION?

☐ After Christ arose and visited earth for forty days, the scripture teaches that he ascended into the presence of God the Father leaving the Holy Spirit upon the earth as a gift and comforter for His people.

• "He that descended is the same also that ascended up far above all heavens, that he might fill all things." Ephesians 4:10

• "This Jesus hath God raised up, whereof we all are witnesses. Therefore being by the right hand of God exalted, and having received of the Father the promise of the Holy Ghost, he hath shed forth this, which ye now see and hear." Acts 2:32-33

☐ Christ ascended to "sit at the right hand of God the Father" This scriptural expression means that Christ returned to the Father and therefore occupies all power and all authority. His current activity is to eternally make intercession for us [believers] as the High Priest in the Holy Temple of God. This is the purpose of the incarnation, death, burial, resurrection and ascension of Christ. As a result of this we have a plan available to be made righteous in the eyes of God the Father, be restored and live unto Him as a family, be made a kingdom of priests, chosen unto him to serve him and to be a praise unto him for his glory!

• "Which he wrought in Christ, when he raised him from the dead, and set him at his own right hand in the heavenly places, Far above all principality, and power, and might, and dominion, and every name that is named, not only in this world, but also in that which is to come: And hath put all things under his feet, and gave him to be the head over all things to the church, Which is his body, the fulness of him that filleth all in all." Ephesians 1:20-23

• "And that he died for all, that they which live should not henceforth live unto themselves, but unto him which died for them, and rose again." 2 Corinthians 5:15

• "Who is he that condemneth? It is Christ that died, yea rather, that is risen again, who is even at the right hand of God, who also maketh intercession for us." Romans 8:34

Chapter 16
RECEIVING CHRIST AS LORD
(Salvation)

108. IS THIS "ALL" OF SALVATION; THE INCARNATION, THE REDEMPTION, THE RESURRECTION AND THE ASCENSION?

☐ NO. Believing is the first step, but it is not all of salvation. An individual must not only believe but he must act on that which he declares to believe by receiving. This is called the "doing" or proof of his believing. "Doing" is the test of true faith or belief in any principle.

109. HOW DO I ACTIVATE MY FAITH IN CHRIST?

☐ Recognize your sinful state. Until we receive Christ, we are sinners regardless as to whether or not actual sins were committed. This is true because of the original sin of disobedience that took place in the Garden of Eden. All men thereafter were born in sin [transgression of the Law].

> • "For all have sinned, and come short of the glory of God." Romans 3:23

☐ Repent of your sins. This means to become sorry in your heart for the sin(s); so sorry that there is a willingness to change and completely turn from the actual sin in your life.

> •"In meekness instructing those that oppose themselves; if God peradventure will give them repentance to the acknowledging of the truth; And that they may recover themselves out of the snare of the devil, who are taken captive by him at his will." 2 Timothy 2:25-26

☐ Confess your sins before God. Ask his forgiveness for those specific sins that you remember and admitting your desire to be cleansed also of the original corruption of your nature as a result of the sin of Adam and Eve.

> • "Against thee, thee only, have I sinned, and done this evil in thy sight: that thou mightest be justified when thou speakest, and be clear when thou judgest. Behold, I was shapen in iniquity, and in sin did my mother conceive me." Psalms 51:4-5

> • "If we confess our sins, he is faithful and just to forgive us our sins, and to cleanse us from all unrighteousness." 1 John 1:9

☐ Accept Christ as the sacrifice for sin through believing in his blood as the only ransom for man's sin.

> • "Much more then, being now justified by his blood, we shall be saved from wrath through him." Romans 5:9

> • "Whom God hath set forth to be a propitiation through faith in his blood, to declare his righteousness for the remission of sins that are past, through the forbearance of God; To declare, I say, at this time his righteousness: that he might be just, and the justifier of him which believeth in Jesus." Romans 3:25-26

☐ Believe that God has accepted your repentance, confession, and faith in the life and shed blood of Jesus, His Son, as your ransom for the sin penalty. Believe that he also accepts your faith in his birth [incarnation], death, and resurrection as the redemptive plan of God for mankind. Knowing then that God accepts your faith in him, ask him to come in and dwell in your heart. This prayer he will gladly hear. His delight is to respond to your invitation. You will then experience what is commonly called the "new birth experience" or being "born again". Your heart becomes filled with love for God, his ways, his people, and you become a member of His royal family!

> • "But what saith it? The word is nigh thee, even in thy mouth, and in thy heart: that is, the word of faith, which we preach; That if thou shalt confess with thy mouth the

Lord Jesus, and shalt believe in thine heart that God hath raised him from the dead, thou shalt be saved. For with the heart man believeth unto righteousness; and with the mouth confession is made unto salvation." Romans 10:8-10

• "Whom God hath set forth to be a propitiation through faith in his blood, to declare his righteousness for the remission of sins that are past, through the forbearance of God; To declare, I say, at this time his righteousness: that he might be just, and the justifier of him which believeth in Jesus." Romans 3:25-26

• "And this is the confidence that we have in him, that, if we ask any thing according to his will, he heareth us: And if we know that he hear us, whatsoever we ask, we know that we have the petitions that we desired of him." 1 John 5:14-15

• "And what agreement hath the temple of God with idols? for ye are the temple of the living God; as God hath said, I will dwell in them, and walk in them; and I will be their God, and they shall be my people." 2 Corinthians 6:16

Chapter 17
THE NEW COVENANT
(God's Commitment to Me)

110. WHAT DOES IT MEAN TO BE IN CHRIST?

☐ Being in Christ, belonging to Christ, actually means to be in covenant relationship with him.

111. WHAT IS THE NEW COVENANT?

☐ The New Covenant is the compact or agreement God wants mankind in this generation to respond to. It was made before the foundations of the world were made between God the Father and Christ Jesus the Son. It was initiated at the crucifixion of Christ. It's simply SALVATION through the crucifixion of Christ, who purchased redemption for mankind through his death.

☐ Christ wants you to contract or agree (make covenant) with him in salvation and all that comes as a result of it.

• "But now hath he obtained a more excellent ministry, by how much also he is the mediator of a better covenant, which was established upon better promises." Hebrews 8:6

112. WHAT ARE THE BLESSINGS OF THE NEW COVENANT?

☐ Pardon for sin. Remission for the penalty of sin through Jesus!

• "To him give all the prophets witness, that through his name whosoever believeth in him shall receive remission of sins." Acts 10:43

☐ Justification. A declaration of right standing (righteousness) before God!

> • "Therefore being justified by faith, we have peace with God through our Lord Jesus Christ." Romans 5:1

☐ Adoption. We are placed as sons into the family of God!

> • "For ye have not received the spirit of bondage again to fear; but ye have received the Spirit of adoption, whereby we cry, Abba, Father." Romans 8:15

☐ Glorification. Man fell from the glory of God in the Garden of Eden. The new covenant brings the believer back into the glory of God!

> • "And the glory which thou gavest me I have given them; that they may be one, even as we are one." John 17:22

☐ Healing & Miracles.

☐ Resurrection. Christ was the resurrection and the life, the conqueror of death We experience a (spiritual) resurrection from death to life when we receive Christ.

> • "Verily, verily, I say unto you, He that heareth my word, and believeth on him that sent me, hath everlasting life, and shall not come into condemnation; but is passed from death unto life. Verily, verily, I say unto you, The hour is coming, and now is, when the dead shall hear the voice of the Son of God: and they that hear shall live. For as the Father hath life in himself; so hath he given to the Son to have life in himself; And hath given him authority to execute judgment also, because he is the Son of man. Marvel not at this: for the hour is coming, in the which all that are in the graves shall hear his voice, And shall come forth; they that have done good, unto the resurrection of life; and they that have done evil, unto the resurrection of damnation." John 5:24-29

> • "And you hath he quickened, who were dead in trespasses and sins: Wherein in time past ye walked

according to the course of this world, according to the prince of the power of the air, the spirit that now worketh in the children of disobedience: Among whom also we all had our conversation in times past in the lusts of our flesh, fulfilling the desires of the flesh and of the mind; and were by nature the children of wrath, even as others. But God, who is rich in mercy, for his great love wherewith he loved us." Ephesians 2:14

☐ Table of the Lord. The broken bread and wine are symbols of the New Covenant sacrifice of Jesus. When we gather at the Table of the Lord there are blessings of unity and strength available to receive. Any and all needs can/should be received by faith as the communing is taking place!

> • "For I have received of the Lord that which also I delivered unto you, That the Lord Jesus the same night in which he was betrayed took bread: And when he had given thanks, he brake it, and said, Take, eat: this is my body, which is broken for you: this do in remembrance of me." 1 Corinthians 11:23-34

☐ Security. We have the confirmation of the Spirit that we are walking in truth, this makes us secure and gives us assurance of our salvation and covenant with God!

> • "And hereby we know that we are of the truth, and shall assure our hearts before him." 1 John 3:19

☐ Out Poured Spirit. The prophets of the Old Covenants spoke of the time where there would be an out pouring of the Spirit; we are experiencing the blessings by living in fulfilled prophesy!

> • "And it shall come to pass afterward, that I will pour out my spirit upon all flesh;

and your sons and your daughters shall prophesy, your old men shall dream dreams, your young men shall see visions: And also upon the servants and upon the handmaids in those days will I pour out my spirit." Joel 2:28-29

113. WHAT ARE THE DIVINE EXPRESSIONS OF OUR COVENANT?

☐The three divine components or expressions of our covenant are:

• The WORD (promises) of the Covenant. God the Father is the initiator or maker of the covenant. Our covenant is the commitment of the Father's Word to us. He declares he would send His Son to redeem mankind.

• The BLOOD of the Covenant. This was the Son's work for us, the sacrifice of His body and life. He became the mediator or living (human) substance of the words of God. Without the shedding of blood there would be no remission of sin; therefore, our covenant cannot be authentic without the blood.

• The SEAL of the Covenant. The Holy Spirit "seals" the covenant agreement. His function is to carry out the Will of the Father through Christ the Son. He is the executer, finisher, and sealer of this covenant. After Christ had fulfilled His function, in his fleshly body, the completion of the work had to be worked out through mankind. The Holy Spirit (The Comforter), as the quickening power of God was sent to abide and guide mankind forever.

114. DOES A "NAME" OR "SIGNATURE' HAVE ANY SIGNIFICANCE OR VALUE RELATIVE TO A COVENANT?

☐ YES. When any agreement or covenant is drawn between two parties, it is not authentic, real, or even recognized as having any value without a name or signature attached. This is also true with divine covenants as well. God's "name" is his confirmation that he will be to the covenant partner all that he says he will be and provide for all their necessary needs. He revealed His name(s) [characteristic qualities] to various men throughout time in the Bible. He usually called Himself "Jehovah ___________". Jehovah means "Lord God". The Lord God (Jehovah) covenants (by signature of His Name[s]) to be active on our behalf in the following ways below. These are called the Jehovahistic names of God or His Covenant/Redemptive names:

- *Jehovah Adonai*, The Lord God My Master
- *Jehovah Jireh*, The Lord God My Provider
- *Jehovah Nissi,* The Lord God My Banner
- *Jehovah Rapha*, The Lord God My Healer
- *Jehovah Shaphat,* The Lord God Is Judge
- *Jehovah Elyon*, The Lord God Most High
- *Jehovah Gibbor,* The Lord God Mighty
- *Jehovah Hosenu*, The Lord God My Maker
- *Jehovah Elohim Saboath*, The Lord God of Hosts
- *Jehovah Tsidkenu*, The Lord God My Righteousness
- *Jehovah Shammah*, The Lord God Everpresent
- *Jehovah Mekaddeskum*, The Lord God My Sanctifier
- *Jehovah Shalom*, The Lord God My Peace
- *Jehovah Rohi*, The Lord God My Shepherd
- *Jehovah Elohim*, The Lord God My Redeemer
- *Jehovah Kanna*, The Lord God A Jealous God

Chapter 18
MINE BECAUSE I'M HIS
(Benefits of Belonging)

115. ARE THERE BENEFITS OF BEING A SON OF GOD?

☐ Yes. Once you belong to God He is there to be a Father to you in more ways that your natural Father can.

116. WHAT ARE SOME OF THE BENEFITS OF BEING SAVED IN CHRIST?

☐ We have more than just this temporal life; we will live eternally. Even in death, we live.

• "Verily, verily, I say unto you, He that heareth my word, and believeth on him that sent me, hath everlasting life, and shall not come into condemnation; but is passed from death unto life." John 5:24

• "For God so loved the world, that he gave his only begotten Son, that whosoever believeth in him should not perish, but have everlasting life." John 3:16

☐ We have healing for our bodies because Christ bore our infirmities on Calvary, taking stripes on his back to benefit us.

• "Who his own self bare our sins in his own body on the tree, that we, being dead to sins, should live unto righteousness: by whose stripes ye were healed." 1 Peter 2:24

• "That it might be fulfilled which was spoken by Esaias the prophet, saying, Himself took our infirmities, and bare our sicknesses." Matthew 8:17

☐ Our sins are remitted. We are righteous (cleansed) by the shedding of his blood for our lives.

> • "If we confess our sins, he is faithful and just to forgive us our sins, and to cleanse us from all unrighteousness." 1 John 1:9

> • "Come now, and let us reason together, saith the LORD: though your sins be as scarlet, they shall be as white as snow; though they be red like crimson, they shall be as wool." Isaiah 1:18

> • "For this is my blood of the new testament, which is shed for many for the remission of sins." Matthew 26:28

☐ We have become are the children of God! We are different from other people in that we are the heirs of God and shall also be glorified with Him.

> • "The Spirit itself beareth witness with our spirit, that we are the children of God: And if children, then heirs; heirs of God, and joint heirs with Christ; if so be that we suffer with him, that we may be also glorified together." Romans 8:16-17

☐ We are not ruined by the iniquities of our forefathers. These are the sins of our forefathers passed onto us from previous generations or inherited weaknesses. We can therefore offer the promise and hope to our children to be delivered of these things.

> • "Who is a God like unto thee that pardoneth iniquity, and passeth by the transgression of the remnant of his heritage? he retaineth not his anger for ever, because he delighteth in mercy. He will turn again, he will have compassion upon us; he will subdue our iniquities; and thou wilt cast all their sins into the depths of the sea." Micah 7:18-19

> • "And I will cleanse them from all their iniquity, whereby they have sinned against me; and I will

pardon all their iniquities, whereby they have sinned, and whereby they have transgressed against me." Jeremiah 33:8

☐ We are at peace with God. We also have the peace of God in our lives in the midst of distress, grief, death, and all adverse circumstances.

- "And the peace of God, which passeth all understanding, shall keep your hearts and minds through Christ Jesus." Philippians 4:7

- "Therefore being justified by faith, we have peace with God through our Lord Jesus Christ." Romans 5:1

- "Yea, though I walk through the valley of the shadow of death, I will fear no evil: for thou art with me; thy rod and thy staff they comfort me." Psalms 23:4

☐ A disciple has the power to live free of fear. He recognizes the power of His God to do all things and subdue all things even through using the believer. Disciples can therefore walk in full confidence and strength.

- "Thou wilt keep him in perfect peace, whose mind is stayed on thee: because he trusteth in thee." Isaiah 26:3

- "Peace I leave with you, my peace I give unto you: not as the world giveth, give I unto you. Let not your heart be troubled, neither let it be afraid." John 14:27

- "For God hath not given us the spirit of fear; but of power, and of love, and of a sound mind." 2 Timothy 1:7

117. HOW ARE WE EQUIPPED TO MASTER THE "TRICKS" AND CUNNING EVIL WAYS OF SATAN AND HIS DEMONS TODAY?

☐ Disciples are to wear the whole armor of the God. This is our guard against the wickedness of Satan and his demons. These armor items are:

- Truth for your loins (belt about your waist).
- Righteousness (right standing with God in holiness) for your breastplate.
- Peace (the good news of the gospel of peace) for your feet.
- Faith (your sturdy belief in God, His Word, and all that pertains to His teachings) for a shield.
- Salvation (knowing you have been redeemed by the blood of Jesus) as your helmet.
- The Word of God as your sword.

- "Finally, my brethren, be strong in the Lord, and in the power of his might. Put on the whole armour of God, that ye may be able to stand against the wiles of the devil." Ephesians 6:10-11

Chapter 19
THE SIX FOUNDATION STONES

118. WHAT ARE THE SIX FOUNDATION STONES?

☐ The six foundation stones are fundamental groundwork experiences required of each disciple by God for building toward maturity. These stones are:

- Repentance from dead works
- Faith toward God
- Doctrine of Baptisms: [Water, Holy Spirit, and Baptism of Fire]
- Laying on of Hands
- Resurrection of the Dead
- Eternal Judgment

• "Therefore leaving the principles of the doctrine of Christ, let us go on unto perfection; not laying again the foundation of repentance from dead works, and of faith toward God, Of the doctrine of baptisms, and of laying on of hands, and of resurrection of the dead, and of eternal judgment." Hebrews 6:1-2

119. WHAT IS REPENTANCE?

☐ The word "repentance" means to turn, change one's mind from something. Repentance is actually accepting full responsibility for what you have done or for what state you are in (spiritually), then making the decision and resulting action to make a change which moves you in a totally new direction. Repentance is making the decision to turn from sin and (human) works and return to God.

• "That ye put off concerning the former conversation the old man, which is corrupt according to the deceitful lusts." Ephesians 4:22

• "Then Peter said unto them, Repent, and be baptized every one of you in the name of Jesus Christ for the remission of sins, and ye shall receive the gift of the Holy Ghost." Acts 2:38

• "Repent ye therefore, and be converted, that your sins may be blotted out, when the times of refreshing shall come from the presence of the Lord." Acts 3:19

☐ In Luke 15:11 32, the parable of the Prodigal Son is an excellent example of true repentance. Three key points to the parable are listed below:

• The son thought about his condition (came to his senses). Verse 17.

• He willed to act upon what he knew was right (made up his mind to do it). ... "I will get up and return to my father"...Verse 18.

• He followed through with his decision to change by acting .... "He came to his father's house"... Verse 20.

120. WHAT ARE DEEDS OR FRUIT OF REPENTANCE?

☐ If you have made a true change and turned to God, you will show "deeds" or "fruit" of repentance according to Acts 26:20; "Therefore bring forth fruit in keeping with repentance." Some fruit of repentance are:

• Hatred of Sin
• Totally forsaking Sin
• Godly sorrow for Sin
• Freedom from Sin

• "Knowing this, that our old man is crucified with him, that the body of sin might be destroyed, that henceforth we should not serve sin." Romans 6:6

• "Now I rejoice, not that ye were made sorry, but that ye sorrowed to repentance: for ye were made sorry after a godly manner, that ye might receive damage by us in nothing. For godly sorrow worketh repentance to salvation not to be repented of: but the sorrow of the world worketh death." 2 Corinthians 7:9-10

• "Thou hast loved righteousness, and hated iniquity; therefore God, even thy God, hath anointed thee with the oil of gladness above thy fellows." Hebrews 1:9

121. WHAT IS REPENTANCE FROM DEAD WORKS?

☐ Dead Works are our attempting to continue to fulfill religious laws, activities, or works of the flesh in our own strength and ability instead of relying upon God's source and power through us. These works are usually handed down to us from the traditions (ways) of men. God is not pleased through dead works nor can they make us acceptable unto Him. Only the blood of Jesus can! We are only required to respond to the Word of God and NOT the opinions of man.

• "Forasmuch as ye know that ye were not redeemed with corruptible things, as silver and gold, from your vain conversation received by tradition from your fathers." 1 Peter 1:18-19

• "Howbeit in vain do they worship me, teaching for doctrines the commandments of men. For laying aside the commandment of God, ye hold the tradition of men, as the washing of pots and cups: and many other such like things ye do. And he said unto them, Full well ye reject the commandment of God, that ye may keep your own tradition." Mark 7:7-9

> • "But we are all as an unclean thing, and all our righteousnesses are as filthy rags; and we all do fade as a leaf; and our iniquities, like the wind, have taken us away." Isaiah 64:6

122. HOW DO I LAY THE PRINCIPLE OF REPENTANCE FROM DEAD WORKS IN MY LIFE?

☐ In order to experience this principle in your life, you need only to:

> • Read and understand what God's Word says about repentance from dead works.
> • Believe what God's Word says about repentance from dead works.
> • Recognize your need to align your life up with the written word since God has made it real to you.
> • Confess (repent) your willingness to God to tear down everything you have built up in your life contrary to His Word in this area.
> • Apply the Word as it is written repent and turn determine to CHANGE.
> • Receive your deliverance from God and continue in God's Word that the fruit of change will continually manifest itself in your life.

123. WHAT IS FAITH?

☐ Faith is the NOW substance (active and believing) of our relationship with God and all he promises for us in His Word. In simple form we can say faith is to believe God without question or doubt. It is firm persuasion, assurance, and trust. Faith is the foundation of the entire Christian life.

> • "Now faith is the substance of things hoped for, the evidence of things not seen." Hebrews 11:1

> • "For we walk by faith, not by sight." 2 Corinthians 5:7

• "Jesus saith unto her, Said I not unto thee, that, if thou wouldest believe, thou shouldest see the glory of God?" John 11:40

• "But without faith it is impossible to please him: for he that cometh to God must believe that he is, and that he is a rewarder of them that diligently seek him." Hebrews 11:6

124. WHAT IS THE SOURCE OF REAL FAITH?

☐ The source of real faith is the receiving of the Word of God, whether spoken, written or prophetic utterance. Faith comes by hearing the word of God (Romans 10:17). So by hearing the word of God we can receive faith to believe God for salvation and anything else we need once in Him.

• "So then faith cometh by hearing, and hearing by the word of God." Romans 10:17

• "But hath in due times manifested his word through preaching, which is committed unto me according to the commandment of God our Savior." Titus 1:3

125. WHAT DOES IT MEAN TO BE JUSTIFIED BY FAITH?

☐ We are justified (made in right standing with God) by faith when we accept the favor and mercy of God through redemption provided for us in Christ. Through the shedding of his blood (life giving sacrifice), we are free from the penalty of sin. Our lives are new before the Lord as if we were never separated from God. Thus we are justified; restored to righteousness as in the beginning as if we never sinned.

> • "Being justified freely by his grace through the redemption that is in Christ Jesus: Whom God hath set forth to be a propitiation through faith in his blood, to declare his righteousness for the remission of sins that are past, through the forbearance of God; To declare, I say, at this time his righteousness: that he might be just, and the justifier of him which believeth in Jesus." Romans 3:24-26

> • "For by grace are ye saved through faith; and that not of yourselves: it is the gift of God: Not of works, lest any man should boast." Ephesians 2:8-9

> • "Who was delivered for our offences, and was raised again for our justification." Romans 4:25

126. WHAT IS FAITH TOWARD GOD?

☐ Faith toward God is the faith to believe God for salvation based on hearing and responding to the Gospel. This faith stems from the heart and produces a righteous in your life. It causes you to believe God unquestionably. The foundation of Faith Toward God is established in the heart of an individual when he responds and acts toward God with this faith which will free him from the bondage of sin.

> • "But what saith it? The word is nigh thee, even in thy mouth, and in thy heart: that is, the word of faith, which we preach; That if thou shalt confess with thy mouth the Lord Jesus, and shalt believe in thine heart that God hath raised him from the dead, thou shalt be saved. For with the heart man believeth unto righteousness; and with the mouth confession is made unto salvation ... For whosoever shall call upon the name of the Lord shall be saved." Romans 10:8-10, 13

127. WHAT IS SALVATION?

☐ Salvation is our acceptance by God into "sonship" with Him and the assurance of eternal life. This is based on believing [having faith] in the Lord Jesus Christ and receiving His total redemptive work for our life in that Christ DIED for our sins, he was BURIED, he ROSE AGAIN on the third day, and he RETURNED to God the Father

☐ To lay the fundamental truth of Faith Toward God, one must not only believe for salvation but must also confess [say and speak] that Jesus is Lord of their life. Without believing, receiving and confession, there will be no results of eternal salvation.

> • "But what saith it? The word is nigh thee, even in thy mouth, and in thy heart: that is, the word of faith, which we preach." Romans 10:8

> • "If we confess our sins, he is faithful and just to forgive us our sins, and to cleanse us from all unrighteousness." 1 John 1:9

> • "He that covereth his sins shall not prosper: but whoso confesseth and forsaketh them shall have mercy." Proverbs 28:13

> • "Whosoever therefore shall confess me before men, him will I confess also before my Father which is in heaven. But whosoever shall deny me before men, him will I also deny before my Father which is in heaven." Matthew 10:32-33

128. IS THE DOCTRINE OF FAITH TOWARD GOD NECESSARY FOR ALL MEN?

☐ YES. All men need to lay this foundation in their lives. Because of the original sin of Adam [disobedience] in

the Garden of Eden all men were born in sin. This sin separates man from God. Man must understand that only through having faith in God can man be justified. So all men must by faith accept the redemptive work of Christ Jesus in order to have relationship with God the Father. Accepting this redemption rids man of the curse of sin, death and eternal separation from God.

129. DOES BELIEVING GOD FOR SALVATION ENCOMPASS THE COMPLETE DOCTRINE OF FAITH TOWARD GOD?

☐ NO. We can receive nothing from God except by faith. Everything we will need from God such as healing, deliverance, comfort, blessings, etc., requires us to exercise our faith to receive from God.

130. WHAT'S THE NEXT STEP AFTER ACCEPTING CHRIST THROUGH FAITH?

☐ The next step is to submit yourself to water baptism. In water baptism we identify with the death, burial and resurrection of Christ Jesus. Our corrupt nature [the old man, hostility], which dwelt within us because of the original sin of Adam, is removed from us in water baptism.

131. WHAT IS WATER BAPTISM?

☐ Water Baptism is the simple immersing [plunging of the body into fluid so as to completely cover] of a person into water. Physically the individual is completely submerged into the water. While being submerged, God completes a spiritual operation within the spiritual heart of the person.

132. WHAT TAKES PLACE "SPIRITUALLY" IN WATER BAPTISM?

☐ When baptized, we are being baptized into Christ's death. So that as he was crucified and went to the grave, we in turn die to our own selfish desires and ways as we go into the liquid grave [water of baptism]. Baptism destroys the body of sin, the "old man", so that we, AFTER baptism might not serve sin which intends to enslave us in it. We become free from its grips. Baptism removes the penalty of sin which is death and frees us by giving us life in Christ. Then just as Christ was raised and was glorified, we come up from the waters of baptism and walk in the newness of life, not yielding to the "old man", but to the "man" glorified after Christ. This "new man" is not a slave to sin, but one who walks in righteousness.

> • "Know ye not, that so many of us as were baptized into Jesus Christ were baptized into his death? Therefore we are buried with him by baptism into death: that like as Christ was raised up from the dead by the glory of the Father, even so we also should walk in newness of life. For if we have been planted together in the likeness of his death, we shall be also in the likeness of his resurrection: Knowing this, that our old man is crucified with him, that the body of sin might be destroyed, that henceforth we should not serve sin." Romans 6:3-6

> • "Among whom also we all had our conversation in times past in the lusts of our flesh, fulfilling the desires of the flesh and of the mind; and were by nature the children of wrath, even as others." Ephesians 2:3

> • "Therefore if any man be in Christ, he is a new creature: old things are passed away; behold, all things are become new." 2 Corinthians 5:17

133. WHAT IS THE OLD MAN?

☐ The "old man" is the corrupt nature that is in us before baptism. This nature is the result of the original sin of disobedience of Adam. He is the unregenerate man, deceitful and full of every lust and sin.

> • "And unto Adam he said, Because thou hast hearkened unto the voice of thy wife, and hast eaten of the

tree, of which I commanded thee, saying, Thou shalt not eat of it: cursed is the ground for thy sake; in sorrow shalt thou eat of it all the days of thy life." Genesis 3:17

• "And unto Adam he said, Because thou hast hearkened unto the voice of thy wife, and hast eaten of the tree, of which I commanded thee, saying, Thou shalt not eat of it: cursed is the ground for thy sake; in sorrow shalt thou eat of it all the days of thy life." Ephesians 4:22

134. I'VE HEARD OF "HEART CIRCUMCISION". WHAT DOES THIS MEAN?

□ It's simply a phrase that makes reference to the spiritual operation that takes place in the waters of baptism where the original sinful nature of a person [hostility] is removed as they are buried with Christ in the water. When they rise from the water God has performed this spiritual operation called "heart circumcision" on them and they will be a "new" man at peace with God.

• "In whom also ye are circumcised with the circumcision made without hands, in putting off the body of the sins of the flesh by the circumcision of Christ: Buried with him in baptism, wherein also ye are risen with him through the faith of the operation of God, who hath raised him from the dead." Colossians 2:11-12

• "For he is not a Jew, which is one outwardly; neither is that circumcision, which is outward in the flesh: But he is a Jew, which is one inwardly; and circumcision is that of the heart, in the spirit, and not in the letter; whose praise is not of men, but of God." Romans 2:28-29

135. IS HEART CIRCUMCISION [BAPTISM] A NECESSARY PART OF THE "NEW BIRTH" EXPERIENCE?

☐ YES. You really can't experience the nature of Christ without having the hostility of the original sin removed. Since this removing of the hostility against God takes place in water baptism, you must follow Christ's command to be baptized in order to PUT ON CHRIST. It is through this baptism that we actually exchange the old nature for the new man, thereby putting on Christ.

> • "For as many of you as have been baptized into Christ have put on Christ. There is neither Jew nor Greek, there is neither bond nor free, there is neither male nor female: for ye are all one in Christ Jesus." Galatians 3:27-28

> • "Therefore if any man be in Christ, he is a new creature: old things are passed away; behold, all things are become new." 2 Corinthians 5:17

136. DOES MY AGE MATTER?

☐ NO. The only biblical restriction placed upon baptism is that an individual must be able to confess and accept Christ as the one Lord and Savior with revealed understanding, sincerity and faith. Upon this confession of faith he can go on to "put on Christ" through heart circumcision in water baptism.

> • "He saith unto them, But whom say ye that I am? And Simon Peter answered and said, Thou art the Christ, the Son of the living God. And Jesus answered and said unto him, Blessed art thou, Simon Barjona: for

flesh and blood hath not revealed it unto thee, but my Father which is in heaven." Matthew 16:15-17

137. INTO WHAT NAME OR TITLE AM I TO BE BAPTIZED?

□ Jesus instructed his disciples to baptize in the "NAME" [singular] of the Father, Son and Holy Ghost. The "NAME" for the titles of Father, Son and Holy Ghost is the LORD JESUS CHRIST. In this name was the fullness of the power of the Godhead given. Power was not given to titles, but to the God man Jesus Christ.

> • "Go ye therefore, and teach all nations, baptizing them in the name of the Father, and of the Son, and of the Holy Ghost." Matthew 28:19

> • "For in him dwelleth all the fulness of the Godhead bodily. And ye are complete in him, which is the head of all principality and power." Colossians 2:9-10

> • "Therefore let all the house of Israel know assuredly, that God hath made that same Jesus, whom ye have crucified, both Lord and Christ. Then Peter said unto them, Repent, and be baptized every one of you in the name of Jesus Christ for the remission of sins, and ye shall receive the gift of the Holy Ghost." Acts 2:36, 38

> • "And whatsoever ye do in word or deed, do all in the name of the Lord Jesus, giving thanks to God and the Father by him." Colossians 3:17

> • "And Jesus came and spake unto them, saying, All power is given unto me in heaven and in earth." Matthew 28:18

□ Peter and the disciples had the full revelation of what Jesus meant when he instructed them to baptize in the "NAME" of the Father, Son and Holy Ghost. They were not confused with John's baptism [the Baptist] which was for repentance to prepare the way of Jesus the Messiah. Neither should we.

> • "And he said unto them, Unto what then were ye baptized? And they said, Unto John's baptism. Then said Paul, John verily baptized with the baptism of repentance, saying unto the people that they should believe on him, which should come after him, that is, on Christ Jesus." Acts 19:3-4

☐ The disciples understood that when Jesus paid the price for man's redemption through his death, burial and resurrection that HE alone ushered the way for mankind into a new covenant with an inward work of heart circumcision. Therefore they baptized believers in the name of the LORD JESUS CHRIST. The Early Church also followed this pattern ... so should we.

> • "Therefore let all the house of Israel know assuredly, that God hath made that same Jesus, whom ye have crucified, both Lord and Christ." Acts 2:36

> • "Know ye not, that so many of us as were baptized into Jesus Christ were baptized into his death?" Romans 6:3

> • "And it came to pass, that, while Apollos was at Corinth, Paul having passed through the upper coasts came to Ephesus: and finding certain disciples, He said unto them, Have ye received the Holy Ghost since ye believed? And they said unto him, We have not so much as heard whether there be any Holy Ghost. And he said unto them, Unto what then were ye baptized? And they said, Unto John's baptism. Then said Paul, John verily baptized with the baptism of repentance, saying unto the people, that they should believe on him which should come after him, that is, on Christ Jesus. When they heard this, they were baptized in the name of the Lord Jesus. And

when Paul had laid his hands upon them, the Holy Ghost came on them; and they spake with tongues, and prophesied. And all the men were about twelve." Acts 19:1-7

• "While Peter yet spake these words, the Holy Ghost fell on all them which heard the word. And they of the circumcision which believed were astonished, as many as came with Peter, because that on the Gentiles also was poured out the gift of the Holy Ghost. For they heard them speak with tongues, and magnify God. Then answered Peter, Can any man forbid water, that these should not be baptized, which have received the Holy Ghost as well as we? And he commanded them to be baptized in the name of the Lord. Then prayed they him to tarry certain days." Acts 10:44-48

138. WHAT DOES IT MEAN TO BE BAPTIZED IN THE HOLY GHOST?

☐ In this baptism, the believer is to be immersed, submerged and covered with the Holy Spirit, which is the abiding presence and power of God. It's God pouring forth and out from Himself His Spirit upon/into the receiving believer until he's overflowing or filled with His Presence. This baptism provides the believer with an over whelming entrance into the spiritual realm.

• "And it shall come to pass afterward, that I will pour out my spirit upon all flesh; and your sons and your daughters shall prophesy, your old men shall dream dreams, your young men shall see visions." Joel 2:28 or Acts 2:17

• "But ye shall receive power, after that the Holy Ghost is come upon you: and ye shall be witnesses unto me both in Jerusalem, and in all Judaea, and in Samaria, and unto the uttermost part of the earth." Acts 1:8

139. DID JESUS SPEAK OF THE HOLY GHOST?

☐ YES. The Holy Ghost or Holy Spirit was promised by Jesus as a gift of from God the Father for us.

- "And, behold, I send the promise of my Father upon you: but tarry ye in the city of Jerusalem, until ye be endued with power from on high." Luke 24:49

- "Then Peter said unto them, Repent, and be baptized every one of you in the name of Jesus Christ for the remission of sins, and ye shall receive the gift of the Holy Ghost." Acts 2:38

- "For John truly baptized with water; but ye shall be baptized with the Holy Ghost not many days hence." Acts 1:5

140. WHAT OTHER EXPRESSIONS ARE USED TO REFER TO THE HOLY SPIRIT?

☐ *The Spirit of Truth*

- "If ye love me, keep my commandments. And I will pray the Father, and he shall give you another Comforter, that he may abide with you forever; Even the Spirit of truth; whom the world cannot receive, because it seeth him not, neither knoweth him: but ye know him; for he dwelleth with you, and shall be in you. I will not leave you comfortless: I will come to you. Yet a little while, and the world seeth me no more; but ye see me: because I live, ye shall live also." John 14:15-19

☐ *The Helper*

> • "But the Comforter, which is the Holy Ghost, whom the Father will send in my name, he shall teach you all things, and bring all things to your remembrance, whatsoever I have said unto you." John 14:26

☐ *Living Water*

> • "He that believeth on me, as the scripture hath said, out of his belly shall flow rivers of living water." John 7:38

☐ *Spirit of Christ [or the Son]*

> • "But ye are not in the flesh, but in the Spirit, if so be that the Spirit of God dwell in you. Now if any man have not the Spirit of Christ, he is none of his." Romans 8:9

> • "And because ye are sons, God hath sent forth the Spirit of his Son into your hearts, crying, Abba, Father." Galatians 4:6

141. GOD GAVE US THE HOLY SPIRIT FOR WHAT REASONS?

☐ To give believers the boldness to witness to others about Jesus.

> • "But ye shall receive power, after that the Holy Ghost is come upon you: and ye shall be witnesses unto me both in Jerusalem, and in all Judaea, and in Samaria, and unto the uttermost part of the earth." Acts 1:8

☐ To equip the believer to do uncommon things [supernatural] for God's Glory.

> • "And these signs shall follow them that believe; In my name shall they cast out devils; they shall speak with new tongues; They shall take up serpents;

and if they drink any deadly thing, it shall not hurt them; they shall lay hands on the sick, and they shall recover." Mark 16:17-18

☐ To "seal" the believer. According to the Smith's Bible Dictionary there was a great importance attached to a "seal" in the eastern countries. Without one, no document was regarded as authentic [real]. Today, with documents, we look for a personal notarized signature as the "seal" or authenticity that a person agrees with the terms and agreements of a document. In past times, the "signet ring" was considered the person's "seal" and was an ordinary part of a man's items carried with him. This signet was considered the emblem of authority in Egypt, Persia and the other countries mentioned in the Book of Genesis. Likewise, the Holy Spirit is our "seal" of authenticity. He abides with and among us, everywhere we go. He equips us to live an effective life for Christ. He is the authority for the believer and the Church.

> • "In whom ye also trusted, after that ye heard the word of truth, the gospel of your salvation: in whom also after that ye believed, ye were sealed with that holy Spirit of promise." Ephesians 1:13

☐ To be THE TEACHER of the Church; the "revealer" of the things of God, presently and in the future.

> • "Howbeit when he, the Spirit of truth, is come, he will guide you into all truth: for he shall not speak of himself; but whatsoever he shall hear, that shall he speak: and he will show you things to come." John 16:13

> • "But the Comforter, which is the Holy Ghost, whom the Father will send in my name, he shall teach you all things, and bring all things to your remembrance, whatsoever I have said unto you." John 14:26

☐ To intercede for the believer in prayer. We are able to pray in tongues after we've received the Baptism in the Holy Spirit.

- "Likewise the Spirit also helpeth our infirmities: for we know not what we should pray for as we ought: but the Spirit itself maketh intercession for us with groanings which cannot be uttered. And he that searcheth the hearts knoweth what is the mind of the Spirit, because he maketh intercession for the saints according to the will of God." Romans 8:26-27

☐ To enable us to praise, sing and worship in a deeper spiritual realm.

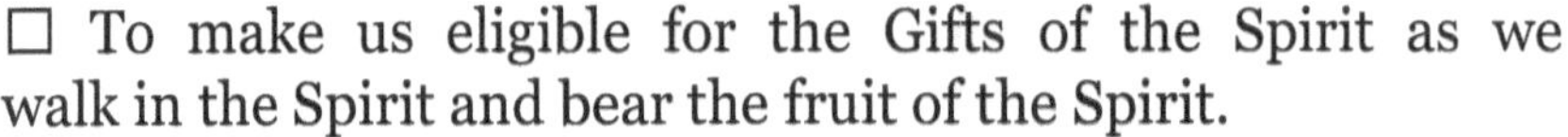

- "Saying, I will declare thy name unto my brethren, in the midst of the church will I sing praise unto thee." Hebrews 2:12

- "What is it then? I will pray with the spirit, and I will pray with the understanding also: I will sing with the spirit, and I will sing with the understanding also." 1 Corinthians 14:15

☐ To make us eligible for the Gifts of the Spirit as we walk in the Spirit and bear the fruit of the Spirit.

- "That in every thing ye are enriched by him, in all utterance, and in all knowledge; Even as the testimony of Christ was confirmed in you: So that ye come behind in no gift; waiting for the coming of our Lord Jesus Christ." 1 Corinthians 1:5-7

- "Follow after charity, and desire spiritual gifts, but rather that ye may prophesy." 1 Corinthians 14:1

142. IS THE HOLY SPIRIT FOR EVERYONE?

☐ NO. God calls whom He wills into His Kingdom. God, as promised, sent the Holy Spirit to every believer and convert. All believers should receive and be baptized in the Holy Spirit!

> • "For the promise is unto you, and to your children, and to all that are afar off, even as many as the Lord our God shall call." Acts 2:39

143. DON'T I RECEIVE GOD'S SPIRIT WHEN I REPENT OR EXPERIENCE THE "NEW BIRTH"?

☐ The Baptism in the Holy Spirit is the FULLEST, most complete experience of the Spirit. When one experiences repentance he can be assured that the Spirit of God is "with" him [in measure]; however Jesus and his disciples made a clear distinction in the scripture between the "Spirit" experience of repentance and the "Spirit" experience as in the Baptism of the Holy Spirit, which is the INDWELLING of the Spirit inside you [until you inwardly overflow]. The scriptures show these separate experiences:

☐ *John baptized with water, but Christ was to come to baptize with the Holy Spirit.*

> • "And, being assembled together with them, commanded them that they should not depart from Jerusalem, but wait for the promise of the Father, which, saith he, ye have heard of me. For John truly baptized with water; but ye shall be baptized with the Holy Ghost not many days hence. When they therefore were come together, they asked of him, saying, Lord, wilt thou at this time restore again the kingdom to Israel?" Acts 1:4-6

☐ *The disciples had already repented and the Spirit of God was with them, but they were also instructed to wait to receive the Baptism in the Holy Spirit, the INDWELLING.*

> • "And, being assembled together with them, commanded them that they should not depart from Jerusalem, but wait for the promise of the Father, which, saith he, ye have heard of me." Acts 1:4

□ *The fullness of the Spirit was sent from God as they were gathered together on the day of Pentecost. They received a new experience that day evidenced by speaking with new tongues.*

> • "And they were all filled with the Holy Ghost, and began to speak with other tongues, as the Spirit gave them utterance." Acts 2:4

144. HOW DO I RECEIVE THE BAPTISM OF THE HOLY SPIRIT?

□ If you have obeyed the command of Christ to repent and be water baptized, you qualify to receive the Holy Ghost. Ask God to fill you with the Holy Ghost. Read the following scriptures below to prepare your heart to receive the Holy Ghost:

> • "Then Peter said unto them, Repent, and be baptized every one of you in the name of Jesus Christ for the remission of sins, and ye shall receive the gift of the Holy Ghost." Acts 2:38

> • "If ye then, being evil, know how to give good gifts unto your children: how much more shall your heavenly Father give the Holy Spirit to them that ask him?" Luke 11:13

> • "And we are his witnesses of these things; and so is also the Holy Ghost, whom God hath given to them that obey him." Acts 5:32

> • "He that speaketh in an unknown tongue edifieth himself; but he that prophesieth edifieth the church." 1 Corinthians 14:4

• "In the law it is written, With men of other tongues and other lips will I speak unto this people; and yet for all that will they not hear me, saith the Lord." 1 Corinthians 14:21

• "For with stammering lips and another tongue will he speak to this people." Isaiah 28:11

☐ One way to receive the Holy Spirit is through the laying on of an anointed believer's hands

> • "Now when the apostles which were at Jerusalem heard that Samaria had received the word of God, they sent unto them Peter and John: Who, when they were come down, prayed for them, that they might receive the Holy Ghost: (For as yet he was fallen upon none of them: only they were baptized in the name of the Lord Jesus.) Then laid they their hands on them, and they received the Holy Ghost. And when Simon saw that through laying on of the apostles' hands the Holy Ghost was given, he offered them money, Saying, Give me also this power, that on whomsoever I lay hands, he may receive the Holy Ghost." Acts 8:14-19

☐ God's sovereign baptism [God baptizes you without any human coaching or involvement].

> • And suddenly there came a sound from heaven as of a rushing mighty wind, and it filled all the house where they were sitting. And there appeared unto them cloven tongues like as of fire, and it sat upon each of them. And they were all filled with the Holy Ghost, and began to speak with other tongues, as the Spirit gave them utterance." Acts 2:2-4

> • "While Peter yet spake these words, the Holy Ghost fell on all them which heard the word. And they of the circumcision which believed were astonished, as many as came with Peter, because that on the Gentiles

also was poured out the gift of the Holy Ghost. For they heard them speak with tongues, and magnify God..." Acts 10:44-46

☐ The necessary actions to receive from God are:

• *Ask the Lord to baptize you.* Relax as you do this, just open your spirit to receive this gift by giving thanks and praise to God. Become engrossed in your communication to God.

• *The presence of God, "anointing" or "spirit" of God will come upon you, motivating you to praise Him from deep within.*

• *Anointed believers will lay their hands upon you invoking God's Spirit to flow from them into you.* [If God chooses sovereignty baptizes you, this step is omitted].

• *As His presence surrounds you, you will find yourself tending to praise and worship God in languages/sounds other than English.* The Holy Spirit will give you these "utterings" to speak. Do not look for an emotional or physical feeling. Just speak whatever He gives you to say.

• *Do not try to understand in your mind what you are saying or even how you sound.* To your mind it will sound like you are speaking "gibberish." You are speaking spiritual things, which cannot be understood intellectually. You spirit is communicating directly with God. You must speak these "utterings" by faith. The Holy Spirit will not overpower you. As you speak, your vocal cords and tongue will cooperate with His flowing through you.

☐ Some people choose to receive the Baptism in the Holy Spirit through laborious asking, reverent, agonizing prayer. This has traditionally been called "tarrying". Although God has made this process quite simple a believer need not feel inferior or superior because of the "way" by which he received the baptism. The primary concern of God the Father is that ALL believers receive Him!

145. HOW DO I "KNOW" I HAVE RECEIVED THE HOLY SPIRIT?

☐ According to the scriptures, speaking with "tongues" always accompanies the baptism in the Holy Spirit. It's the evidence of having received His Spirit. As we receive the infilling of His Spirit, tongues will follow spontaneously.

• "And when Paul had laid his hands upon them, the Holy Ghost came on them; and they spake with tongues, and prophesied." Acts 19:6

• "How God anointed Jesus of Nazareth with the Holy Ghost and with power: who went about doing good, and healing all that were oppressed of the devil; for God was with him. And we are witnesses of all things which he did both in the land of the Jews, and in Jerusalem; whom they slew and hanged on a tree: Him God raised up the third day, and showed him openly; Not to all the people, but unto witnesses chosen before of God, even to us, who did eat and drink with him after he rose from the dead. And he commanded us to preach unto the people, and to testify that it is he which was ordained of God to be the

Judge of quick and dead. To him give all the prophets witness, that through his name whosoever believeth in him shall receive remission of sins. While Peter yet spake these words, the Holy Ghost fell on all them which heard the word. And they of the circumcision which believed were astonished, as many as came with Peter, because that on the Gentiles also was poured out the gift of the Holy Ghost. For they heard them speak with tongues, and magnify God." Acts 10:38-46

146. WHAT IS THE BELIEVER'S RESPONSIBILITY AFTER BEING "FILLED"?

☐ After being filled with the Holy Spirit a believer is to make it a daily practice of communicating [praying, praising] in the Spirit [in tongues]. This builds up his faith in being an Effective Witness for Christ, participating in supernatural manifestations, experiencing the power of intercession, becoming an active channel of God's Gifts and Fruit of the Spirit.

• "But ye, beloved, building up yourselves on your most holy faith, praying in the Holy Ghost." Jude 1:20

147. WHAT IS THE BAPTISM OF FIRE?

☐ The baptism of fire is a process God takes his children through for the purpose of separating them unto Himself. God causes them to mature because the individual learns to overcome weak areas in his life. This separating and maturing is brought about through the  persecutions allowed by God to attack the individual's weak areas. When he overcomes these weaknesses he is strengthened.

• "John answered, saying unto them all, I indeed baptize you with water; but one mightier than I cometh, the latchet of whose shoes I am not worthy to unloose: he shall baptize you with the Holy Ghost and with fire: Whose fan is in his hand, and he will thoroughly purge his floor, and will gather the wheat into his garner; but the chaff he will burn with fire unquenchable." Luke 3:16-17

• "I am come to send fire on the earth; and what will I, if it be already kindled? But I have a baptism to be baptized with; and how am I straitened till it be accomplished! Suppose ye that I am come to give peace on earth? I tell you, Nay; but rather division: For from henceforth there shall be five in one house divided, three against two, and two against three." Luke 12:49-52

148. WHEN DOES THE BAPTISM OF FIRE BEGIN IN A BELIEVER'S LIFE?

☐ The baptism of fire begins with receiving the Holy Spirit baptism. There is no mention of the baptism of fire in the scripture unless the baptism in the Holy Spirit is first mentioned.

• "John answered, saying unto them all, I indeed baptize you with water; but one mightier than I cometh, the latchet of whose shoes I am not worthy to unloose: he shall baptize you with the Holy Ghost and with fire: Whose fan is in his hand, and he will thoroughly purge his floor, and will gather the wheat into his garner; but the chaff he will burn with fire unquenchable." Luke 3:16-17

149. DID JESUS UNDERGO THIS BAPTISM?

☐ Yes. Jesus also experienced the baptism of fire. This experience for him was being sent forty [40] days in the wilderness and then being tempted. He was our perfect example. His temptation focused in three areas; lust of the eye; lust of the flesh, and the pride of life. These are also the same "root" areas for our temptations today.

• "And Jesus being full of the Holy Ghost returned from Jordan, and was led by the Spirit into the wilderness, Being forty days tempted of the devil. And in those days he did eat nothing: and when they were ended, he afterward hungered." Luke 4:1-2

• "For all that is in the world, the lust of the flesh, and the lust of the eyes, and the pride of life, is not of the Father, but is of the world." 1 John 2:16

150. WHAT DOES THIS BAPTISM DO FOR US?

☐ The baptism of fire works a wonderful work in our life. It causes the waste [chaff] to be driven from our lives so that we may mature, become polished and effective in our walk, witness [example] to the world.

• "Whose fan is in his hand, and he will thoroughly purge his floor, and will gather the wheat into his garner; but the chaff he will burn with fire unquenchable." Luke 3:17

• "Though he were a Son, yet learned he obedience by the things which he suffered; And being made perfect, he became the author of eternal salvation unto all them that obey him." Hebrews 5:8-9

151. IS THERE ANOTHER WORD IN SCRIPTURE FOR THE BAPTISM OF FIRE?

☐ "Chastening" is another word used in scripture for reference to the baptism of fire. It's the love of God shown through affliction and tribulation, which drives waste [bad character]. This chastening drives the submitted believer towards a close fellowship and relationship with God. God allows us to be chastened because of His love for us and in the end causes us to profit. It is not punishment; for that would be God's expressed wrath or anger. Chastening expresses God's love for us.

> • "For they verily for a few days chastened us after their own pleasure; but he for our profit, that we might be partakers of his holiness. Now no chastening for the present seemeth to be joyous, but grievous: nevertheless afterward it yieldeth the peaceable fruit of righteousness unto them which are exercised thereby." Hebrews 12:10-11

> • "And ye have forgotten the exhortation which speaketh unto you as unto children, My son, despise not thou the chastening of the Lord, nor faint when thou art rebuked of him." Hebrews 12:5

152. WHAT ARE THE MANIFESTATIONS OF THIS BAPTISM?

☐ The manifestations of this baptism are afflictions, trials, persecution, tribulations and sometimes illness. It is important to know that in the process of enduring these afflictions one is made stronger in faith and their spiritual walk [maturity]. Believers are to rejoice when tempted knowing that it works for our profit if we hold fast to the Word of God in the midst.

> • "Many are the afflictions of the righteous: but the LORD delivereth him out of them all." Psalms 34:19

> • "Behold, I have refined thee, but not with silver; I have chosen thee in the furnace of affliction." Isaiah 48:10

☐ When we totally submit to God and trust him to do a work in our lives as He desires; we will come forth as beautiful, clean, and purified as gold. Being tried by the fire as gold, we will be refined!

> • "But he knoweth the way that I take: when he hath tried me, I shall come forth as gold." Job 23:10

> • "Behold, I have refined thee, but not with silver; I have chosen thee in the furnace of affliction." Isaiah 48:10

153. IS THIS CHASTENING AN INSTANT WORK OR IS IT PROGRESSIVE?

☐ We are immediately and instantly cleansed from the filth and bondage of original sin through water baptism; however we must progressively continue to walk with God daily, choosing to walk, do and respond in the way he would desire us to do so. This doing is progressive. The fire will be applied to our lives whenever the need for refinement arises; therefore, our cleansing is progressive and continual throughout life until our rapture. We, by daily living in the Word, grow toward perfection.

> • "And ye shall be holy unto me: for I the LORD am holy, and have severed you from other people, that ye should be mine." Leviticus 20:26

> • "For they verily for a few days chastened us after their own pleasure; but he for our profit, that we might be partakers of his holiness." Hebrews 12:10

> • "The LORD will perfect that which concerneth me: thy mercy, O LORD, endureth for ever: forsake not the works of thine own hands." Psalms 138:8

154. WHAT IS THE DOCTRINE OF THE LAYING ON OF HANDS?

☐ The scriptural doctrine of the laying on of hands is that authority; blessings, spiritual gifts and healings are imparted and/or transmitted through a believer placing his hand upon the head of another individual. Included also in this doctrine is that placing hands on the head of a believer with prayer is a definite act that [through spiritual grace, wisdom and power] sets apart one for a task of service, sends one out for ministry, confirms and establishes doctrine [teaching] in a believer.

> • "And by the hands of the apostles were many signs and wonders wrought among the people; (and they were all with one accord in Solomon's porch." Acts 5:12

> • "And Ananias went his way, and entered into the house; and putting his hands on him said, Brother Saul, the Lord, even Jesus, that appeared unto thee in the way as thou camest, hath sent me, that thou mightest receive thy sight, and be filled with the Holy Ghost." Acts 9:17

> • "And it came to pass, that the father of Publius lay sick of a fever and of a bloody flux: to whom Paul entered in, and prayed, and laid his hands on him, and

> • "Then laid they their hands on them, and they received the Holy Ghost." Acts 8:17

> • "And he took them up in his arms, put his hands upon them, and blessed them." Mark 10:16

155. IS THIS DOCTRINE NEW?

☐ NO. Israel laid hands on Ephraim and Manasseh and blessed them.

> • "And Israel stretched out his right hand, and laid it upon Ephraim's head, who was the younger,

and his left hand upon Manasseh's head, guiding his hands wittingly; for Manasseh was the firstborn." Genesis 48:14

☐Moses transferred his authority to Joshua by the laying on of hands.

> • "And the LORD said unto Moses, Take thee Joshua the son of Nun, a man in whom is the spirit, and lay thine hand upon him; And set him before Eleazar the priest, and before all the congregation; and give him a charge in their sight. And thou shalt put some of thine honour upon him, that all the congregation of the children of Israel may be obedient. And he shall stand before Eleazar the priest, who shall ask counsel for him after the judgment of Urim before the LORD: at his word shall they go out, and at his word they shall come in, both he, and all the children of Israel with him, even all the congregation. And Moses did as the LORD commanded him: and he took Joshua, and set him before Eleazar the priest, and before all the congregation: And he laid his hands upon him, and gave him a charge, as the LORD commanded by the hand of Moses." Numbers 27:18-23

☐ Hands were laid on men as they were set aside for tasks in the Church.

> • "Whom they set before the apostles: and when they had prayed, they laid their hands on them. " Acts 6:6

☐ The laying on of hands was used to send men out of the church for ministry [by God's Spirit].

> • "And when they had fasted and prayed, and laid their hands on them, they sent them away. " Acts 13:3

☐ The laying on of hands was used for impartation of spiritual gifts and the baptism in the Holy Ghost.

> • "And when Paul had laid his hands upon them, the Holy Ghost came on them; and they spake with tongues, and prophesied." Acts 19:6

☐ Jesus laid hands on the sick and healed them and he commissioned the apostles to do the same. The Church of today is an extension of the ministry of the early Church; therefore, she has the same authority and commission.

> • "And besought him greatly, saying, My little daughter lieth at the point of death: I pray thee, come and lay thy hands on her, that she may be healed; and she shall live." Mark 5:23

> • "And they bring unto him one that was deaf, and had an impediment in his speech; and they beseech him to put his hand upon him." Mark 7:32

156. ARE THERE PRECAUTIONS TO ADMINISTERING THE LAYING ON OF HANDS?

☐ Yes...Christ like qualities and characteristics should be apparent before hands are laid on a person. The laying on of hands is to be done prayerfully and not hastily. If this is hastily done the scripture warns and cautions that the one laying the hands on the individual partakes in the responsibility for the sins of the person he lays his hands upon.

> • "Lay hands suddenly on no man, neither be partaker of other men's sins: keep thyself pure." 1 Timothy 5:22

157. WHAT DOES THE DOCTRINE OF RESURRECTION INSTRUCT US TO BELIEVE?

☐ We are to believe that God will raise the dead to life again in either of two [2] separate resurrections; the resurrection of the dead in Christ and the resurrection of the wicked ... at the end of the ages ...

☐ Christ will come from heaven to a level of the earth's atmosphere and call in a shout for "the dead in Christ" to arise. The archangel will accompany him and the trumpet will give a beckoning sound. At that time Christ calls for the dead in him to rise. Those believers who are still alive will be caught up [ascend, rise] to meet the Lord in the earth's atmosphere. This is also termed amongst believers as the "rapture". Those dead and alive believers responding to the command of God will automatically experience a transformation of their bodies into an immortal and incorruptible substance. They will be spirit; glorious and powerful! Those righteous resurrected bodies shall be escorted to paradise [in the presence of God] in the third heaven.

• "For the Lord himself shall descend from heaven with a shout, with the voice of the archangel, and with the trump of God: and the dead in Christ shall rise first: Then we which are alive and remain shall be caught up together with them in the clouds, to meet the Lord in the air: and so shall we ever be with the Lord."
1 Thessalonians 4:16-17

• "Marvel not at this: for the hour is coming, in the which all that are in the graves shall hear his voice, And shall come forth; they that have done good, unto the resurrection of life; and they that have done evil, unto the resurrection of damnation." John 5:28-29

• "Behold, I show you a mystery; We shall not all sleep, but we shall all be changed, In a moment, in the twinkling of an eye, at the last trump: for the trumpet shall sound, and the dead shall be raised incorruptible, and we shall be changed." 1 Corinthians 15:51-52

• "So also is the resurrection of the dead. It is sown in corruption; it is raised in incorruption: It is sown in dishonour; it is raised in glory: it is sown in weakness; it is raised in power: It is sown a natural body; it is raised a spiritual body. There is a natural body, and there is a spiritual body." 1 Corinthians 15:42-44

• "I knew a man in Christ above fourteen years ago, (whether in the body, I cannot tell; or whether out of the body, I cannot tell: God knoweth;) such an one caught up to the third heaven. And I knew such a man, (whether in the body, or out of the body, I cannot tell: God knoweth;) How that he was caught up into paradise, and heard unspeakable words, which it is not lawful for a man to utter." 2 Corinthians 12:2-4

• "But the rest of the dead lived not again until the thousand years were finished. This is the first resurrection. Blessed and holy is he that hath part in the first resurrection: on such the second death hath no power, but they shall be priests of God and of Christ, and shall reign with him a thousand years." Revelation 20:5-6

☐ In the resurrection of the wicked, at the end of the ages, the wicked dead will stand before Jesus Christ before the throne of God [called the Great White Throne] and give an answer for the life they lived and their rejection of Christ. They will not have any excuse or defense for the rejection of Christ and will therefore be sentenced by Christ to eternal death. They will be in a spirit form and be conscious, have memory and experience pain and hurt. This will be the eternal fate for the wicked, an eternal sentence in hell.

• "Marvel not at this: for the hour is coming, in the which all that are in the graves shall hear his voice, And shall come forth; they that have done good, unto the resurrection of life; and they that have done evil, unto the resurrection of damnation." John 5:28-29

• "And I saw a great white throne, and him that sat on it, from whose face the earth and the heaven fled away; and there was found no place for them." Revelation 20:11

• "Blessed and holy is he that hath part in the first resurrection: on such the second death hath no power, but they shall be priests of God and of Christ, and shall reign with him a thousand years ... And whosoever was not found written in the book of life was cast into the lake of fire." Revelation 20:6, 15

• "And the sea gave up the dead which were in it; and death and hell delivered up the dead which were in them: and they were judged every man according to their works." Revelation 20:13

• "He that hath the Son hath life; and he that hath not the Son of God hath not life." 1 John 5:12

158. WHAT DO YOU MEAN ABOUT A THIRD HEAVEN?

☐ In the beginning, God created three heavens. The first heaven is the earth and it's atmosphere, filled with oxygen that is inhabited by Satan & the fallen angels [demons]. The second heaven is known space or solar system where there's no oxygen and weightlessness. God calls the third heaven "paradise." It's the place occupied by believers who've experienced the natural death of the flesh, abiding in the presence of God.

• "How that he was caught up into paradise, and heard unspeakable words, which it is not lawful for a man to utter." 2 Corinthians 12:2-4

159. IS IT NECESSARY TO BELIEVE IN THE RESURRECTION?

☐ Yes...if one rejects the resurrection of Jesus Christ, he refuses to believe the total redemptive work of Christ Jesus died, was buried, arose from the dead and promised the same experience for each of us as believers. Therefore, his salvation is true because scripture specifically says that we must believe this in order to be saved.

• "And if Christ be in you, the body is dead because of sin; but the Spirit is life because of righteousness. But if the Spirit of him that raised up Jesus from the dead dwell in you, he that raised up Christ from the dead shall also quicken your mortal bodies by his Spirit that dwelleth in you." Romans 8:10-11

• "And if Christ be not raised, your faith is vain; ye are yet in your sins." 1 Corinthians 15:17

160. IF WE ARE BORN AGAIN AND NOT PHYSICALLY DEAD, CAN WE EXPERIENCE RESURRECTION?

☐ Yes ... when we were dead in sin and then repented to Christ and received his forgiveness, we received a new life in Christ – a changed life. We were resurrected from a life of spiritual death to one of spiritual life.

• "And you hath he quickened, who were dead in trespasses and sins ... Even when we were dead in sins, hath quickened us together with Christ, (by grace ye are saved;) And hath raised us up together, and made us sit together in heavenly places in Christ Jesus." Ephesians 2:1, 5-6

☐ We also experience resurrection by spiritual warfare through prayer. We change situations and circumstances that would work death in us to those that will work life. Situations that would overcome others or us are changed by our consistency in prayer. We see and experience deliverance in our lives and those we pray for.

• "But we had the sentence of death in ourselves, that we should not trust in ourselves, but in God which raiseth the dead: Who delivered us from so great a death, and doth deliver: in whom we trust that he will yet deliver us."
2 Corinthians 1:9-10

161. WHAT IS ETERNAL JUDGMENT?

☐ It's the belief that every man will eventually have to stand before Christ to account for the things he done in his body and be judged accordingly. Those who've accepted Christ as Lord and Savior will be judged at the Judgment Seat of Christ and those who did not will stand before The Great White Throne for judgment. The decisions rendered at these judgments are eternal.

• "Wherefore we labour, that, whether present or absent, we may be accepted of him. For we must all appear before the judgment seat of Christ; that every one may receive the things done in his body, according to that he hath done, whether it be good or bad. Knowing therefore the terror of the Lord, we persuade men; but we are made manifest unto God; and I trust

also are made manifest in your consciences."
2 Corinthians 5:9-11

162. WHO'S THE JUDGE?

☐ God is the judge of all but He's given the authority to carry out His Judgments to His Son Christ Jesus.

• "To the general assembly and church of the firstborn, which are written in heaven, and to God the Judge of all, and to the spirits of just men made perfect." Hebrews 12:23

• "For the Father judgeth no man, but hath committed all judgment unto the Son: That all men should honour the Son, even as they honour the Father. He that honoureth not the Son honoureth not the Father which hath sent him." John 5:22-23

163. IS THERE A DIFFERENCE BETWEEN THE CONCEPT OF ETERNAL SALVATION AND ETERNAL JUDGMENT?

☐ Yes ... Eternal salvation is determined solely upon the fact of whether an individual has accepted Jesus Christ as Lord and Savior. Your decision of salvation also determines which judgment seat you will stand before in the end. Eternal judgment determines whether you are to be awarded, punished or eternally damned by God – sent to hell.

• "He that hath the Son hath life; and he that hath not the Son of God hath not life." 1 John 5:12

> • "And I say unto you my friends, Be not afraid of them that kill the body, and after that have no more that they can do. But I will forewarn you whom ye shall fear: Fear him, which after he hath killed hath power to cast into hell; yea, I say unto you, Fear him." Luke 12:4-5

164. WHAT IS THIS JUDGMENT SEAT OF CHRIST?

☐ This is the final examination of all believers', whether dead or living, character, stewardship and work to determine their rewards or lost of rewards in the kingdom. What we have done and who we've become will be completely exposed and revealed in His Presence. Those things that are Christ like will be rewarded and those things ungodly will be consumed by fire and we will suffer loss.

> • "For we must all appear before the judgment seat of Christ; that every one may receive the things done in his body, according to that he hath done, whether it be good or bad." 2 Corinthians 5:10

> • "According to the grace of God which is given unto me, as a wise masterbuilder, I have laid the foundation, and another buildeth thereon. But let every man take heed how he buildeth thereupon. For other foundation can no man lay than that is laid, which is Jesus Christ. Now if any man build upon this foundation gold, silver, precious stones, wood, hay, stubble ... If any man's work abide which he hath built thereupon, he shall receive a reward. If any man's work shall be burned, he shall suffer loss: but he himself shall be saved; yet so as by fire." 1 Corinthians 3:10-12, 14-15

165. WHAT IS THE GREAT WHITE THRONE JUDGMENT?

☐ This is the final examination of all non believers, whether living or dead, and will demonstrate the necessity of God's decision of condemnation. Everyone will see in the light of God's perfection "why" his or her deeds were evil. Their own conscience will agree with the condemnation they will receive from God. All will realize why eternal separation from God is absolutely necessary for those who rejected His grace and salvation.

> • "I the LORD search the heart, I try the reins, even to give every man according to his ways, and according to the fruit of his doings." Jeremiah 17:10

> • "In flaming fire taking vengeance on them that know not God, and that obey not the gospel of our Lord Jesus Christ: Who shall be punished with everlasting destruction from the presence of the Lord, and from the glory of his power." 2 Thessalonians 1:8-9

Chapter 20
WALKING IN LOVE
[A Key Fruit of the Spirit]

166. WHY IS LOVE A "KEY" CHARACTERISTIC OF THE FRUIT OF THE SPIRIT?

☐ It was the love of God shown to us by allowing Jesus to go to the cross and die for our salvation. The love God has for mankind is called "agape" and it's undeserved, unprompted, unconditional divine love. Also God IS Love.

• "For God so loved the world, that he gave his only begotten Son, that whosoever believeth in him should not perish, but have everlasting life." John 3:16

• "He that loveth not knoweth not God; for God is love." 1 John 4:8

• "Behold, what manner of love the Father hath bestowed upon us, that we should be called the sons of God: therefore the world knoweth us not, because it knew him not." 1 John 3:1

167. WHAT IS "AGAPE" LOVE?

☐ Agape love is divine love that only comes from God. Listed below are some of its attributes:

☐ Love endures long patient.

• Divine love gives a person the power to be patient to wait. It endows one with the ability to remain in a calm state when situations all around seem to be coming apart. Patience endures the short comings of others and is willing to believe the best of every person. Anyone exercising this characteristic will wait and receive the best from God in His timing rather than settle for the mere satisfaction of taking what we think we may desire when we want to.

☐ Love is kind   kindness.

• Kindness is love activated. Believers who exercise kindness do not willingly hurt others through verbal or physical abuse. To display kindness is to yield to the needs of others by demonstrating Christ as Lord over every situation. It's to respond in a gentleness which springs from the source of a heart changed life.

☐ Love is not jealous does not envy.

• We are to be glad and rejoice for the good blessings of others. In this world where envy and jealousy reign, there is a constant uphill scratch, push, pull down and climb attitude for success or promotion; but in the Church we must understand that promotion comes from the Lord and not the aggressive, ambitious spirit of man. We can then be genuinely happy for others rather than becoming envious.

☐ Love is not proud or conceited humility.

• Pride can destroy all that is good and Christ like in a person making him useless in God's kingdom. God desires to elevate the Church, individually as well as corporately, in power and blessings to serve the world as an equipping force in these latter times. He will pour forth His power only on those who are humble in heart so that only HIS Purposes will be accomplished. Spiritual power and authority in the hands of conceited individuals will destroy many lives because a proud person will always attempt to draw people's heart unto himself rather than to Christ. Humility causes us to honestly realize that in ourselves we are powerless or useless but it's God's power within us that give us the victory. It will cause the world to notice Him as He is revealed through us.

☐ Love does not behave rudely is courteous.

• Our behavior is to display Christ's love for humanity. We are to be courteous and well mannered. The courtesy common to our behavior should not only be the outward "yes madam" and "thank you", but an inward love motivating the polite words that we say. This courtesy becomes a heart generated behavior of love rather than an outward display of goods works! Courtesy should be heart motivated, God inspired and continually displayed in the lives of all of God's people.

☐ Love does not seek it's own way is not selfish.

• The inclinations of natural men are to seek their own way, storming over any obstacle in their way in order to get what they want. Love never seeks her own way. Paul commented on this attitude in his day ... "For all seek after their own interests, not those of Christ Jesus..." [Philippians 2:21]. In Christ, we build for him rather than for ourselves. The key to living an overcoming and unselfish life as a believer is to set your affections on the things of Christ. Do not be overcome by the carnal man who wants to be satisfied by fulfilling self; but rather walk in the spirit and endeavor to please God. It's at the giving up of your own selfishness that your desires are made wholesome and fulfilled in Christ!

☐ Love is not irritable is tempered.

• One operating under divine love will not be irritated easily. He will not allow his temper to control him: therefore peace and temperance will be a way of life for him in every situation. This kind of lifestyle allows for the leading of the Spirit of the Lord as opposed to one's own sensitivity and temper writing his destiny.

☐ Love keeps no record of Evil does not realize that he has been wronged.

• Walking in divine love frees us from fear, suspicion and roots of bitterness. We therefore have no memory [record] of the wrong done to us, but are swift to forgive just as we are forgiven of our sin through Christ. One disciple, named Peter asked Christ how many times we are to forgive. Jesus answered 490 times.

• "Then came Peter to him, and said, Lord, how oft shall my brother sin against me, and I forgive him? till seven times? Jesus saith unto him, I say not unto thee, Until seven times: but, Until seventy times seven." Matthew 18:21-22

☐ Love rejoices not in injustice rejoices in the truth.

• True Godly love does not rejoice in seeing others fail. He is not glad to hear bad reports about others. There is something inwardly wrong with the person who feels joy when he discovers the failure of another person. The love of God encourages and supports a person as long as the individual endeavors to walk in truth. It rejoices when the truth prevails even when it pertains to punishment for crime. There is no compromise in Christ for He is truth.

• "Though I speak with the tongues of men and of angels, and have not charity, I am become as sounding brass, or a tinkling cymbal. And though I have the gift of prophecy, and understand all mysteries, and all knowledge; and though I have all faith, so that I could remove mountains, and have not charity, I am nothing. And though I bestow all my goods to feed the poor, and though I give my body to be burned, and have not charity, it profiteth me nothing. Charity suffereth long, and is kind; charity envieth not; charity vaunteth not itself, is not puffed up, Doth not behave itself unseemly, seeketh not her own, is not easily provoked, thinketh no evil; Rejoiceth not in iniquity, but rejoiceth in the truth; Beareth all things, believeth all things, hopeth all things, endureth all things. Charity never faileth: but whether there be prophecies, they shall fail; whether there be tongues, they shall cease; whether there be knowledge, it shall vanish away." 1 Corinthians 13:1-8

Chapter 21
COMPANIONS
(Friendship)

168. DOES CHRIST SPEAK AGAINST FRIENDSHIP WITH THE WORLD?

☐ Yes he does! No believer is to conform to the world. The Bible states that doing this makes you an enemy of God. It compares friendship with the world as adultery. Christ is the bridegroom of the church, his bride, according to the scriptures. Therefore to befriend the world is to have mixed affairs and relationships with someone other than your own and is also called adultery. Remember, the kind of people with whom you associate will be the kind of people you will be like. You are responsible to pick and choose whom you keep company and fellowship with. This does not mean to totally avoid the non believer because they also need to see the light of Christ in you.

• "Ye adulterers and adulteresses, know ye not that the friendship of the world is enmity with God? whosoever therefore will be a friend of the world is the enemy of God." James 4:4

• "For I am jealous over you with godly jealousy: for I have espoused you to one husband, that I may present you as a chaste virgin to Christ." 2 Corinthians 11:2

169. WHAT IS THE REACTION OF AN UNBELIEVER [HIS ATTITUDE] TOWARD BELIEVERS WHOSE LIVES SPEAK THE LIGHT OF CHRIST?

☐ The scriptures teach that if you live the life of a believer you will be persecuted and hated by the world even as the world hated Christ. True love is foreign to the unbeliever. Darkness cannot comprehend the love of God, neither does it demonstrates it. Based upon these truths, it's impossible to have close companionship with those who are not capable of loving and understanding true friendship. Such relationships will eventually lead to compromise of biblical values for the sake of getting along with another person.

> • "If the world hate you, ye know that it hated me before it hated you." John 15:18-19

> • "And when he had made a scourge of small cords, he drove them all out of the temple, and the sheep, and the oxen; and poured out the changers' money, and overthrew the tables; And said unto them that sold doves, Take these things hence; make not my Father's house an house of merchandise." John 2:15-16

170. DOES THIS MEAN THAT WE SHOULD WITHDRAW FROM THE WORLD AS MUCH AS POSSIBLE AND HAVE NOTHING TO DO WITH UNBELIEVERS?

☐ No! Contrary to popular belief, Christ was our perfect example in this. He mingled with sinners quite freely, but he knew his position and stood fast in the midst of their company so much so that his presence won sinners to God. One of the chief charges the religious leaders made against Jesus was that he ate with sinners.

> • "And when the Pharisees saw it, they said unto his disciples, Why eateth your Master with publicans and sinners? But when Jesus heard that, he said unto them, They that be whole need not a physician, but they that are sick." Matthew 9:11-12

171. HOW DO I MAKE FRIENDS?

☐ Show yourself to be a friendly person approachable. You must be willing to pay the simple price of "being friendly". Certainly there are risks involved of being rejected when you set out to make friends, but doing it God's way makes it worth taking any risks. The biblical way is to expose yourself and be friendly.

- "A man that hath friends must show himself friendly: and there is a friend that sticketh closer than a brother." Proverbs 18:24

172. WHAT KIND OF ATTITUDES SHOULD I HAVE AND DEVELOP IN ORDER TO MAINTAIN FRIENDSHIPS?

☐ Be Loving a friend loves at all times. This means he is able to see the best out of any situation rather than the worst. He is loyal as long as the loyalty does not lead or involve sin.

- Establish loyalty in your friendships. Your friend must know that you can be trusted with concerns dear to his heart. You can prove to be trustworthy by showing consistent loyalty and love at all times.

☐ Be Helpful – a friend helps in the times of need. In fact, he is especially tender and sensitive when the other person of the relationship seems troubled. In the bible, David & Jonathan were the best of friends their souls were knit to each other.

- Be sensitive to the needs of your friend and let him know with words and actions that you are there to help. A true friend is like a close brother when hard times hit he's stands by, upholds and can be depended upon to help.

> • "A friend loveth at all times, and a brother is born for adversity." Proverbs 17:17

☐ Be A Good Listener are you usually listening or talking? Have you developed the quality of being a good listener? Friendships cannot be established when one is determined to do all of the speaking. Allow the other party to talk and listen thoroughly to what is being said. Do not hear with your ears and at the same time be formulating counter thoughts, responses and comments all while the other person is sharing. Hear the other person out completely before speaking. Hear with your heart.

> • Sometimes the counsel of a true friend is the godly advice we need in order to save us from the snare of the evil one. Unless we are attentive, we cannot hear. According to the scripture it's wise to listen to the counsel or advice of our parents and older friends as well.

> • "Ointment and perfume rejoice the heart: so doth the sweetness of a man's friend by hearty counsel. Thine own friend, and thy father's friend, forsake not; neither go into thy brother's house in the day of thy calamity: for better is a neighbour that is near than a brother far off." Proverbs 27:9-10

☐ Realize That Differences Strengthen don't give up on your friendship because of differences you may have with the other party. Many times differences strengthen and cement the relationship. Just be as understanding as possible in the midst of a crisis. Carefully guard your tongue and remember that differences in personality sharpen one another and can be used to create better understandings.

> • "Iron sharpeneth iron; so a man sharpeneth the countenance of his friend." Proverbs 27:17

173. ARE WE TO SEEK FRIENDSHIPS IN CHRIST?

☐ Yes! Every believer desperately needs Christ first as a friend above all others. Through relationship with Him in prayer, fellowship, obedience to his word, etc. you will become more aware of His presence within you at all times and in every situation. Christ must be at the head of your list of friendships. Seek Him and prize Him above all others. He is a friend with whom you can be completely sincere He died for your sins to give you life. You can share your fears, frustrations, secrets and joys with Him. The quality of your relationship with Him determines how you relate towards others.

☐ The greatest display of friendship ever was Christ's demonstration of His love for us when He gave His life for mankind. He willingly laid down his life for both you and I. He so desired relationship and God the Father so desired fellowship that Jesus gave Himself to experience shame, suffering and death to provide a bridge for relationship back with God.

> • "A man that hath friends must show himself friendly: and there is a friend that sticketh closer than a brother." Proverbs 18:24

> • "Greater love hath no man than this, that a man lay down his life for his friends." John 15:13

Chapter 22
SHARING JESUS
(Being A Witness)

174. WHAT DOES "BEING A WITNESS" MEAN?

☐ To be a witness is simply to share Christ. It's the responsibility of every believer to share the wonderful news of Jesus by telling others about the saving grace of Christ. We are to tell our neighbors, family, friends and associates of the deliverance power of Christ whenever the opportunity presents itself.

• "But ye shall receive power, after that the Holy Ghost is come upon you: and ye shall be witnesses unto me both in Jerusalem, and in all Judaea, and in Samaria, and unto the uttermost part of the earth." Acts 1:8

175. WHAT ARE A FEW BRIEF TIPS TO EMPLOY TO HELP ME WITNESS EFFECTIVELY?

☐ Pray allow God to prepare your heart. Your greatest desire for this endeavor is for God to go before you and prepare the way for the Word to be received.

☐ Do Not Argue, salvation is in the person of Christ you are basically introducing individuals to Christ. Many people will know about Jesus but don't know him personally. Present Christ's salvation plan as an open invitation for fellowship and relationship. It's the individual's decision to accept or reject your invitation.

☐ Carry The Right Attitude your mouth and life is to be used as a tool for God's glory. You are sharing Christ to "win" friends for the kingdom of God rather than provoking people to resent the presence and company of believers.

176. WHAT AM I WITNESSING?

☐ You are to witness the "good news" of salvation. This is presented in form below:

> • The one true God [Father, Son and Holy Spirit] of the universe created man as his companion; but the evil one, Satan, convinced man to believe that he could become like God himself in knowledge and wisdom by eating of the forbidden fruit. Man believed the voice of Satan, disobeyed God and sinned. Sin in mankind caused a separation from God. Man could no longer have fellowship with God. Even in death man was doomed to live secluded from God, eternally in a tormenting place called hell. God loved man so much that he activated a plan to redeem mankind he had previously developed should he had sinned. Being God, he knew that man would disobey and sin so He sent His Son Jesus to die a cursed human death on the cross to redeem man. By accepting Christ all men have a way to renew fellowship with God. In accepting Christ, man will now experience the very presence of God on earth and live eternally in peace with God as long as he allows the Word of God to change his life. This has nothing to do with a particular church denomination! All who do accept Christ should attend a local church of His choosing. This is the simple message of salvation, believing, receiving and accepting the work of Jesus Christ for our life.

☐ If the individual accepts your presentation of Christ lead him into accepting salvation through the following steps:

> • Acknowledge that he has sinned based upon the original sin of Adam & Eve.

- "For all have sinned, and come short of the glory of God." Romans 3:23

- "And the publican, standing afar off, would not lift up so much as his eyes unto heaven, but smote upon his breast, saying, God be merciful to me a sinner." Luke 18:13

☐ Repent of the sin(s) he has acknowledged.

- "I tell you, Nay: but, except ye repent, ye shall all likewise perish." Luke 13:3

- "Repent ye therefore, and be converted, that your sins may be blotted out, when the times of refreshing shall come from the presence of the Lord." Acts 3:19

☐ Confess his sins so that the Lord will be released to do the work of salvation promised in His Word.

- "If we confess our sins, he is faithful and just to forgive us our sins, and to cleanse us from all unrighteousness." 1 John 1:9

- "For with the heart man believeth unto righteousness; and with the mouth confession is made unto salvation." Romans 10:10

☐ Forsake the sins of your confession. Sorrow is not enough; we must desire to be rid of it.

- "Let the wicked forsake his way, and the unrighteous man his thoughts: and let him return unto the LORD, and he will have mercy upon him; and to our God, for he will abundantly pardon." Isaiah 55:7

☐ Believe the Word of God in John 3:16 and Romans 10:9 10 which declares your freedom from bondage through Christ.

   • "For God so loved the world, that he gave his only begotten Son, that whosoever believeth in him should not perish, but have everlasting life." John 3:16

   • "That if thou shalt confess with thy mouth the Lord Jesus, and shalt believe in thine heart that God hath raised him from the dead, thou shalt be saved. For with the heart man believeth unto righteousness; and with the mouth confession is made unto salvation." Romans 10:9-10

☐ Receive Christ into your heart through prayer based upon Revelations 3:20 and John 1:11-12.

   • "Behold, I stand at the door, and knock: if any man hear my voice, and open the door, I will come in to him, and will sup with him, and he with me." Revelations 3:20

   • "He came unto his own, and his own received him not. But as many as received him, to them gave he power to become the sons of God, even to them that believe on his name." John 1:11-12

Chapter 23
WORDS
(The Believer's Speech)

177. WHAT ARE WORDS?

☐ Words are the containers of the "power" of God that creates and defines spiritual and physical existence. Words are a gift from God. Talking is the highest form of communication. This was given to mankind and angels. God allows only man to choose his own words. Words, chosen by man, can breed love or contention; embrace or rebuke. God will judge us for our management of this gift of using words.

> • "But I say unto you, That every idle word that men shall speak, they shall give account thereof in the day of judgment. For by thy words thou shalt be justified, and by thy words thou shalt be condemned." Matthew 12:36-37

178. HOW IS MY SPEECH TO BE AS A BELIEVER?

☐ Our speech is to be peaceful, beautiful, positive and full of faith. We are to be certain that when we speak words of beauty and value flow from our lips. They are to be pleasant in the midst of the confusion and anger of a sick world. Our words should bring health and healing to the sick and wounded.

> • "Pleasant words are as an honeycomb, sweet to the soul, and health to the bones." Proverbs 16:24

179. WHAT ARE SOME BENEFITS SEASONED WORDS PROVIDES?

☐ Seasoned word can bring joy. When spoken at the needed time, encouragement and comfort can also be the results of words delivered by the believer. Your words can also be vehicles for making peace. Proverbs 15:1 states that soft words turn away wrath and will build relationships in your home, with your parents and family and with friends and neighbors.

> • "A man hath joy by the answer of his mouth: and a word spoken in due season, how good is it!" Proverbs 15:23

> • "A soft answer turneth away wrath: but grievous words stir up anger." Proverbs 15:1

180. WHAT ARE SOME RESULTS OF HARSH AND ABUSIVE WORDS?

☐ Harsh, abusive words are poisonous and cause conflict in homes, schools and relationships with relatives and friends. These type of words break our relationship with God because we are using words to injure others. God forbids us to be a part of talebearers or slander. The Bible says that gossip and rumors cause wounds that sink into the deep parts of the belly more deadly than a blow with a sword.

> • "And the tongue is a fire, a world of iniquity: so is the tongue among our members, that it defileth the whole body, and setteth fire the course of nature; and it is set on fire of hell. But the tongue can no man tame; it is an unruly evil, full of deadly poison." James 3:6, 8

> • "The words of a talebearer are as wounds, and they go down into the innermost parts of the belly." Proverbs 18:8

181. WHAT DOES THE BIBLE SAY ABOUT LYING?

☐ Lying, or being deceitful is sometimes the easiest way out of trouble for us, but God hates this attitude. It's an abomination or wicked sin before Him. Children, who practice lying, become lying adults. For a person to be free, this sin must be rooted out of their spirit. God demands that we are to be truthful despite the cost to us. It delights the Lord for disciples to deal in truth.

> • "Lying lips are abomination to the LORD: but they that deal truly are his delight." Proverbs 12:22

> • "A lying tongue hateth those that are afflicted by it; and a flattering mouth worketh ruin." Proverbs 26:28

182. DO WORDS CARRY A HIDDEN MESSAGE?

☐ Yes. Though spoken from the mouth, words come from a much deeper source. They reveal what is in the heart. Words have revealing power. The Bible expresses the mouth as the outlet for the human heart.

> • "But those things which proceed out of the mouth come forth from the heart; and they defile the man. For out of the heart proceed evil thoughts, murders, adulteries, fornications, thefts, false witness, blasphemies: These are the things which defile a man: but to eat with unwashen hands defileth not a man." Matthew 15:18-20

183. WHAT DOES GOD REQUIRE OF OUR WORDS AND SPEECH HABITS?

☐ The Bible specifically requires the disciple to speak the truth in love. God expects us to be truthful, sincere, incorrupt and doctrinally sound in our speech habits. He requires us to show the same lifestyle as our words declare.

> • "In all things showing thyself a pattern of good works: in doctrine showing uncorruptness, gravity,

sincerity. Sound speech, that cannot be condemned; that he that is of the contrary part may be ashamed, having no evil thing to say of you." Titus 2:7-8

Chapter 24
OUR EXTENDED FAMILY
(The Body of Christ)

184. WHAT IS THE EXTENDED FAMILY OF GOD?

☐ All those who are born of God are part of the extended family of God. This means those who are redeemed by the blood of Christ by believing in his death, burial and resurrection. This family includes people of God from every country, language and race on earth.

• "And if Christ be not raised, your faith is vain; ye are yet in your sins." 1 Corinthians 15:17

• "For he hath made him to be sin for us, who knew no sin; that we might be made the righteousness of God in him." 2 Corinthians 5:21

• "For God so loved the world, that he gave his only begotten Son, that whosoever believeth in him should not perish, but have everlasting life. For God sent not his Son into the world to condemn the world; but that the world through him might be saved." John 3:16-17

• "Forasmuch as ye know that ye were not redeemed with corruptible things, as silver and gold, from your vain conversation received by tradition from your fathers; But with the precious blood of Christ, as of a lamb without blemish and without spot." 1 Peter 1:18-19

185. IS THE EXTENDED FAMILY THE SAME AS "THE CHURCH"?

☐ Yes. The Church comprises all those who are born of God, who have been redeemed by the blood of Christ by believing in his death, burial and resurrection, inclusive of those sons and daughters of God from every country, language and race on earth. The Church is not a physical edifice but a particular people. All these people worldwide have a common bond CHRIST. All have believed and received Him through faith in his redemptive work of deliverance and salvation. All have accepted Him as Lord. The extended family is His Body, the Church. The Greek word translation for Church is "Ecclesia", meaning "called out". This calls "out" the family of God from the lifestyles of the world to a new lifestyle of the Kingdom of God, which is holy and separated unto Himself. The Bible outlines the requirements of this new lifestyle.

> • "But ye are a chosen generation, a royal priesthood, an holy nation, a peculiar people; that ye should show forth the praises of him who hath called you out of darkness into his marvelous light: Which in time past were not a people, but are now the people of God: which had not obtained mercy, but now have obtained mercy." 1 Peter 2:9-10

> • "How that by revelation he made known unto me the mystery; (as I wrote afore in few words, Whereby, when ye read, ye may understand my knowledge in the mystery of Christ) Which in other ages was not made known unto the sons of men, as it is now revealed unto his holy apostles and prophets by the Spirit; That the Gentiles should be fellowheirs, and of the same body, and partakers of his promise in Christ by the gospel." Ephesians 3:3-6

186. WHAT ARE THE MEMBERS OF THE EXTENDED FAMILY CALLED?

☐ They were called "Abraham's seed", "Israel", "True Jews", "Zion" and the heathens called them "Christians."

> • "And if ye be Christ's, then are ye Abraham's seed, and heirs according to the promise." Galatians 3:29

• "For he is not a Jew, which is one outwardly; neither is that circumcision, which is outward in the flesh: But he is a Jew, which is one inwardly; and circumcision is that of the heart, in the spirit, and not in the letter; whose praise is not of men, but of God." Romans 2:28-29

• "A Song and Psalm for the sons of Korah. Great is the LORD, and greatly to be praised in the city of our God, in the mountain of his holiness. Beautiful for situation, the joy of the whole earth, is mount Zion, on the sides of the north, the city of the great King." Psalms 48:1-2

• "And when he had found him, he brought him unto Antioch. And it came to pass, that a whole year they assembled themselves with the church, and taught much people. And the disciples were called Christians first in Antioch." Acts 11:26

•"Then Agrippa said unto Paul, Almost thou persuadest me to be a Christian." Acts 26:28

187. WHAT IS MT. ZION?

□ Mt. Zion was the capital city of King David in the bible. It was the place where he set up a tent of worship as a place for the people to praise God. The place is called the celebrated mountain in Jerusalem. It was geographically the highest land elevation in the far south of the city.

188. WHY WAS IT KNOWN AS "THE CITY OF DAVID"?

□ The land was once occupied by the Canaanites, an enemy of God's people. During the time of David's reign as king, he captured the city from the enemy, enlarged the city and fortified it. It then became known as his city.

189. WHAT DOES THE WORD "ZION" MEAN?

☐ Bible dictionaries and resources express the word "zion" to mean: "high sunny, fortified, fortress, lofty and elevated." This word also suggests political and religious themes. The political themes were that the:

• Old Testament suggests KINGSHIP. The laws and government of the nation of Israel during the reign of David were set forth from Zion in Jerusalem David being a type [example] of Christ.

• New Testament suggests that JESUS CHRIST IS THE KING. Under the new covenant order Christ is THE KING in the [church] city of God. He is the King of Zion. He rules, reign over our lives and we see his government in our lives as we submit our lives to His Word.

• "For unto us a child is born, unto us a son is given: and the government shall be upon his shoulder: and his name shall be called Wonderful, Counsellor, The mighty God, The everlasting Father, The Prince of Peace. Of the increase of his government and peace there shall be no end, upon the throne of David, and upon his kingdom, to order it, and to establish it with judgment and with justice from henceforth even forever. The zeal of the LORD of hosts will perform this. The Lord sent a word into Jacob, and it hath lighted upon Israel. And all the people shall know, even Ephraim and the inhabitant of Samaria, that say in the pride and stoutness of heart." Isaiah 9:6-9

• "Which in his times he shall show, who is the blessed and only Potentate, the King of kings, and Lord of lords." 1 Timothy 6:15

☐ The religious themes were that the:

• Old Testament suggests PRIESTHOOD. The tent of David was the center of the religious capital of the nation in Jerusalem. Those coming into the presence of God would be blessed spiritually.

• New Testament suggests JESUS CHRIST IS HIGH PRIEST AND KING. Christ is our high priest, therefore he is the center of our affairs, the leader of those redeemed. From him flows all we need spiritually. We do not need to look to a fleshly high priest as our ancestors did, but to Christ who is our eternal mediator and the center of our lives. No longer is Zion on a hill in Jerusalem, but Zion is the believer and the dwelling place of the Lord Jesus Christ - the Church.

• "Saying, I will declare thy name unto my brethren, in the midst of the church will I sing praise unto thee." Hebrews 2:12

• "I will declare thy name unto my brethren: in the midst of the congregation will I praise thee." Psalms 22:22

190. SINCE "ZION" IS REALLY GOD'S CHURCH, WHAT ARE SOME OF ITS FACTS?

☐ The KING lives in Zion. David was the King in Mt. Zion, but in the new covenant we apply the psalms specifically to Christ. He is the KING in Zion, the one who is on the throne of His Church and our lives.

☐ The Lord reigns in Zion.

• "The LORD shall reign for ever, even thy God, O Zion, unto all generations. Praise ye the LORD." Psalms 146:10

☐ Singing and shouting should take place in Zion.

   • "Cry out and shout, thou inhabitant of Zion: for great is the Holy One of Israel in the midst of thee." Isaiah 12:6

☐ God [the Father] loves Zion.

   • "A Psalm or Song for the sons of Korah. His foundation is in the holy mountains. The LORD loveth the gates of Zion more than all the dwellings of Jacob. Glorious things are spoken of thee, O city of God. Selah." Psalms 87:1-3

☐ The beauty of God is to shine through Zion.

   • "Out of Zion, the perfection of beauty, God hath shined." Psalms 50:2

☐ Good tidings are carried by Zion. Disciples are to cause the good news of salvation to go forth by their words of life.

   • "O Zion, that bringest good tidings, get thee up into the high mountain; O Jerusalem, that bringest good tidings, lift up thy voice with strength; lift it up, be not afraid; say unto the cities of Judah, Behold your God!" Isaiah 40:9

191. DOES ZION REFER TO SOMETHING IN THE FUTURE?

☐ Yes. The term "Mount Zion" refers to heavenly Zion as well.

   • "And I looked, and, lo, a Lamb stood on the mount Sion, and with him an hundred forty and four thousand, having his Father's name written in their foreheads." Revelation 14:1

• "But ye are come unto mount Sion, and unto the city of the living God, the heavenly Jerusalem, and to an innumerable company of angels." Hebrews 12:22

192. CAN ANYONE BECOME A MEMBER OF THE "EXTENDED FAMILY OF GOD", "THE CHURCH", OR "ZION"?

☐ Yes. Salvation is available for all who will receive Christ. Receiving Christ ushers one into the extended family of God. Personal salvation is experienced by an individual's repentance and simple faith toward God.

• "If we confess our sins, he is faithful and just to forgive us our sins, and to cleanse us from all unrighteousness." 1 John 1:9

• "Wherefore, as by one man sin entered into the world, and death by sin; and so death passed upon all men, for that all have sinned." Romans 5:12

• "For by one Spirit are we all baptized into one body, whether we be Jews or Gentiles, whether we be bond or free; and have been all made to drink into one Spirit." 1 Corinthians 12:13

• "Now when they heard this, they were pricked in their heart, and said unto Peter and to the rest of the apostles, Men and brethren, what shall we do? Then Peter said unto them, Repent, and be baptized every one of you in the name of Jesus Christ for the remission of sins, and ye shall receive the gift of the Holy Ghost." Acts 2:37-38

193. DOES WATER BAPTISM PLAY A PART IN BEING A MEMBER OF GOD'S EXTENDED FAMILY?

☐ Yes. The decision of whether or not to submit to water baptism is basically the difference between "seeing" and "entering into" the benefits of God's Kingdom. Water baptism is a command from Christ to all disciples. A disciple expresses his faith in Christ and his commands through obedience and submission. If an individual will not submit and be obedient to Christ's commands he has no "revelation" or true conviction of WHO Christ is; therefore his repentance and faith is of dead works and his life will not be marked with the spiritual relationship and experiences described in the scriptures.

> • "Jesus answered and said unto him, Verily, verily, I say unto thee, Except a man be born again, he cannot see the kingdom of God." John 3:3

> • "He that believeth and is baptized shall be saved; but he that believeth not shall be damned." Mark 16:16

> • "Then they that gladly received his word were baptized: and the same day there were added unto them about three thousand souls." Acts 2:41

194. DOES THE "CHURCH" FUNCTION SEPARATELY FROM CHRIST?

☐ No. Christ is the head of the Church, his family. All authorities, ministries (services) and individuals function by the governing authority of Christ, who is the Head of the Church.

> • "And he is the head of the body, the church: who is the beginning, the firstborn from the dead; that in all things he might have the preeminence." Colossians 1:18

> • "But speaking the truth in love, may grow up into him in all things, which is the head, even Christ: From whom the whole body fitly joined together and compacted by that which every joint supplieth, according

to the effectual working in the measure of every part, maketh increase of the body unto the edifying of itself in love." Ephesians 4:15-16

195. WHAT ARE SOME OF GOD'S DESIRES FOR HIS CHURCH?

☐ God desires his members (the Church) to have genuine care, concern and support for one another.

- "That there should be no schism in the body; but that the members should have the same care one for another. And whether one member suffer, all the members suffer with it; or one member be honoured, all the members rejoice with it." 1 Corinthians 12:25-26

☐ God desires his members to have genuine love one for the other.

- "We know that we have passed from death unto life, because we love the brethren. He that loveth not his brother abideth in death." 1 John 3:14

- "He that loveth his brother abideth in the light, and there is none occasion of stumbling in him. But he that hateth his brother is in darkness, and walketh in darkness, and knoweth not whither he goeth, because that darkness hath blinded his eyes." 1 John 2:10-11

☐ God wants His people to create individually and corporately a sincere, pure type atmosphere of worship conducive for Him to dwell in their midst. In His dwelling and fellowshipping amongst us, we are blessed, healed, strengthened, changed and renewed.

- "And I heard a great voice out of heaven saying, Behold, the tabernacle of God is with men, and he will dwell with them, and they shall be his people, and God himself shall be with them, and be their God." Revelation 21:3

• "He that dwelleth in the secret place of the most High shall abide under the shadow of the Almighty. I will say of the LORD, He is my refuge and my fortress: my God; in him will I trust. Surely he shall deliver thee from the snare of the fowler, and from the noisome pestilence. He shall cover thee with his feathers, and under his wings shalt thou trust: his truth shall be thy shield and buckler. Thou shalt not be afraid for the terror by night; nor for the arrow that flieth by day; Nor for the pestilence that walketh in darkness; nor for the destruction that wasteth at noonday. A thousand shall fall at thy side, and ten thousand at thy right hand; but it shall not come nigh thee. Only with thine eyes shalt thou behold and see the reward of the wicked. Because thou hast made the LORD, which is my refuge, even the most High, thy habitation; There shall no evil befall thee, neither shall any plague come nigh thy dwelling. For he shall give his angels charge over thee, to keep thee in all thy ways. They shall bear thee up in their hands, lest thou dash thy foot against a stone. Thou shalt tread upon the lion and adder: the young lion and the dragon shalt thou trample under feet. Because he hath set his love upon me, therefore will I deliver him: I will set him on high, because he hath known my name. He shall call upon me, and I will answer him: I will be with him in trouble; I will deliver him, and honour him. With long life will I satisfy him, and show him my salvation." Psalms 91:1-16

196. ONCE I BECOME A MEMBER OF THE UNIVERSAL CHURCH, WITH "WHOM" SHOULD I FELLOWSHIP?

☐ When you are "born again" into God's Kingdom, God also places you into a local church to grow and develop. The bulk of your fellowship should be with fellow disciples. You should only fellowship with the world's followers with the intent of winning them to Christ either by the witness of your conversation or your life.

• "For he is our peace, who hath made both one, and hath broken down the middle wall of partition between us; Having abolished in his flesh the enmity, even the law of commandments contained in ordinances; for to make in himself of twain one new man, so making peace; And that he might reconcile both unto God in one body by the cross, having slain the enmity thereby: And came and preached peace to you which were afar off, and to them that were nigh. For through him we both have access by one Spirit unto the Father. Now therefore ye are no more strangers and foreigners, but fellow citizens with the saints, and of the household of God." Ephesians 2:14-19

• "I wrote unto you in an epistle not to company with fornicators: Yet not altogether with the fornicators of this world, or with the covetous, or extortioners, or with idolaters; for then must ye needs go out of the world. But now I have written unto you not to keep company, if any man that is called a brother be a fornicator, or covetous, or an idolater, or a railer, or a drunkard, or an extortioner; with such an one no not to eat." 1 Corinthians 5:9-11

Chapter 25
THE LOCAL FAMILY OF GOD
(The Local Church Fellowship)

197. WHAT IS THE LOCAL FAMILY OF GOD?

☐ The local family of God comprise of members of the universal body of Christ who dwell in a local vicinity. Cincinnati, Huntsville and Atlanta are local cities in their respective states. Writers of the scripture addressed letters to certain local families in various areas. Most towns and cities had one local body of disciples, however today there are many local churches in one vicinity.

- "Paul, and Silvanus, and Timotheus, unto the church of the Thessalonians which is in God the Father and in the Lord Jesus Christ: Grace be unto you, and peace, from God our Father, and the Lord Jesus Christ." 1 Thessalonians 1:1

- "Unto the church of God which is at Corinth, to them that are sanctified in Christ Jesus, called to be saints, with all that in every place call upon the name of Jesus Christ our Lord, both theirs and ours." 1 Corinthians 1:2

- "And all the brethren which are with me, unto the churches of Galatia." Galatians 1:2

- "Paul and Timotheus, the servants of Jesus Christ, to all the saints in Christ Jesus which are at Philippi, with the bishops and deacons." Philippians 1:1

198. WHAT IS A LOCAL CHURCH FELLOWSHIP?

☐ A local church fellowship is a group of members of the body of Christ who gather together in a local building in a particular community for the purpose of sharing the message of the gospel the common bond of the local fellowship and the extended family.

> • "Saying, I will declare thy name unto my brethren, in the midst of the church will I sing praise unto thee." Hebrews 2:12

> • "For where two or three are gathered together in my name, there am I in the midst of them." Matthew 18:20

199. WHY SHOULD A DISCIPLE BELONG TO A LOCAL CHURCH FAMILY?

☐ The local church provides a place for development, maturity and growing up spiritually. God has set leaders in the local assembly to aid in their growth.

> • "And he gave some, apostles; and some, prophets; and some, evangelists; and some, pastors and teachers; For the perfecting of the saints, for the work of the ministry, for the edifying of the body of Christ: Till we all come in the unity of the faith, and of the knowledge of the Son of God, unto a perfect man, unto the measure of the stature of the fulness of Christ: That we henceforth be no more children, tossed to and fro, and carried about with every wind of doctrine, by the sleight of men, and cunning craftiness, whereby they lie in wait to deceive; But speaking the truth in love, may grow up into him in all things, which is the head, even Christ." Ephesians 4:11-15

☐ It's in the local church family where we learn the necessity of accepting responsibility such as: submitting to authority, giving yourself to the needs of others, being loyal, commitment and faithfulness.

> • "Obey them that have the rule over you, and submit yourselves: for they watch for your souls, as they that must give account, that they may do it with joy, and not with grief: for that is unprofitable for you." Hebrews 13:17

• "Now I say, That the heir, as long as he is a child, differeth nothing from a servant, though he be lord of all; But is under tutors and governors until the time appointed of the father." Galatians 4:1-2

200. WHAT HAPPENS TO THOSE WHO LEARN TO SUBMIT, GIVE OF THEMSELVES AND BE FAITHFUL?

☐ Disciples who master these and other virtues mature in the things of God. God can trust them with more tasks, responsibility and authority as they continue to grow in Him. They will not stagger in the way of godliness, but will be firm in their stand and walk for Christ. These individuals will also manifest or show the world through their lives of being living examples of the glory of God.

• "Neither is there any creature that is not manifest in his sight: but all things are naked and opened unto the eyes of him with whom we have to do. Seeing then that we have a great high priest, that is passed into the heavens, Jesus the Son of God, let us hold fast our profession. For we have not an high priest which cannot be touched with the feeling of our infirmities; but was in all points tempted like as we are, yet without sin." Ephesians 4:13-15

• "For I reckon that the sufferings of this present time are not worthy to be compared with the glory which shall be revealed in us. For the earnest expectation of the creature waiteth for the manifestation of the sons of God." Romans 8:18-19

• "He that is faithful in that which is least is faithful also in much: and he that is unjust in the least is unjust also in much. If therefore ye have not been faithful in the unrighteous mammon, who will commit to your trust the true riches? And if ye have not been faithful in that which is another man's, who shall give you that which is your own?" Luke 16:10-12

• "And he said unto him, Well, thou good servant: because thou hast been faithful in a very little, have thou authority over ten cities." Luke 19:17

Chapter 26
FOOTWASHING
(Washing Thy Brother's Feet)

201. WHAT IS FOOTWASHING?

☐ It is brothers and sisters washing each other's feet in love. Water is poured into a basin and each individual ministers prayer as he washes the other's feet. This is also a time to relieve feelings of anger and offence between one another – individuals will go to the person of offence and make amends. Usually the men will wash the men's feet and the women will wash other women's feet. If there's restoration to be made between opposite sexes such as, male vs female, one person [brother] will make amends personally with his sister and then will ask another female member to wash her feet in his stead. This is done to avoid any opportunities of sexual temptations or seductions.

> • "He riseth from supper, and laid aside his garments; and took a towel, and girded himself. After that he poureth water into a basin, and began to wash the disciples' feet, and to wipe them with the towel wherewith he was girded." John 13:4-5

> • "Let all things be done decently and in order." 1 Corinthians 14:40

202. IS FOOTWASHING SCRIPTURAL?

☐ Yes. Jesus washed his disciples' feet. Jesus, being our example, commanded us that we should wash one another's feet.

203. WHY DID JESUS WASH HIS DISCIPLES' FEET?

☐ Jesus wanted to stress the need for his disciples "to become servants" to one another. The disciples, like most of us, had no natural desire to serve one another to give themselves as a help to one another, but rather they desired to lord over one another to be "chief". Jesus requires us not to think highly of ourselves, but to minister [serve] one another in love. Washing another's feet humbles us and cultivates our love that we may truly become servants one to another.

☐ Jesus also instituted footwashing to teach one another an unforgettable lesson on love. Footwashing demonstrates the true love of the believer for Christ and the brethren. Without it there is hostilities, anger, disunity and a body that will not function properly. With footwashing there is unity, effective ministry, unselfishness and willingness to serve others.

> • "For I say, through the grace given unto me, to every man that is among you, not to think of himself more highly than he ought to think; but to think soberly, according as God hath dealt to every man the measure of faith." Romans 12:3

> • "And he sat down, and called the twelve, and saith unto them, If any man desire to be first, the same shall be last of all, and servant of all." Mark 9:35

> • "But it shall not be so among you: but whosoever will be great among you, let him be your minister; And whosoever will be chief among you, let him be your servant: Even as the Son of man came not to be ministered unto, but to minister, and to give his life a ransom for many." Matthew 20:26-28

204. WHAT IS TO BE THE "ATTITUDE" OF A SERVANT?

☐ A true servant should operate with the attitude of love in his heart.

• "So after he had washed their feet, and had taken his garments, and was set down again, he said unto them, Know ye what I have done to you? Ye call me Master and Lord: and ye say well; for so I am. If I then, your Lord and Master, have washed your feet; ye also ought to wash one another's feet. For I have given you an example, that ye should do as I have done to you ... A new commandment I give unto you, That ye love one another; as I have loved you, that ye also love one another. By this shall all men know that ye are my disciples, if ye have love one to another." John 13:12-15, 34-35

• "And how shall they preach, except they be sent? as it is written, How beautiful are the feet of them that preach the gospel of peace, and bring glad tidings of good things!" Romans 10:15

• "For now we see through a glass, darkly; but then face to face: now I know in part; but then shall I know even as also I am known." 1 Corinthians 13:12

205. CAN I IGNORE PRACTICING FOOTWASHING AND STILL PLEASE THE LORD?

☐ No, you cannot. Peter is an example from scripture of one who did not feel it necessary to wash another's feet. Jesus quickly told Peter that if he did not share in footwashing that Jesus would have no communion or fellowship with him. Peter changed his attitude about footwashing immediately! Because Christ dwells in an atmosphere of love and operates all things by love, he will not commune with individuals who will not sanctify themselves through the ministering of footwashing.

• "Peter saith unto him, Thou shalt never wash my feet. Jesus answered him, If I wash thee not, thou hast no part with me. Simon Peter saith unto him, Lord, not my feet only, but also my hands and my head." John 13:8-9

206. IS THERE ANY CORRELATION OF FOOTWASHING IN THE OLD TESTAMENT?

☐ Yes. The priests who served in the Tabernacle of Moses had to be cleansed regularly in a brass "Laver". Their feet and hands would become wounded and contaminated in the service of preparing fleshly offerings for the brazen altar so they had to repeatedly go to the Laver for washing. God has made a way for our inner wounds and contaminations to be healed and cleansed and continue to walk in perfected love with God the Father and the brethren. Just as we agree to continue in remembrance of the blood of Christ through communion [The Lord's Supper], we continue the water experience [cleansing], not by baptism only but by footwashing as well.

• "And the LORD spake unto Moses, saying, Thou shalt also make a laver of brass, and his foot also of brass, to wash withal: and thou shalt put it between the tabernacle of the congregation and the altar, and thou shalt put water therein. For Aaron and his sons shall wash their hands and their feet thereat: When they go into the tabernacle of the congregation, they shall wash with water, that they die not; or when they come near to the altar to minister, to burn offering made by fire unto the LORD: So they shall wash their hands and their feet, that they die not: and it shall be a statute for ever to them, even to him and to his seed throughout their generations." Exodus 30:17-21

• "For there are three that bear record in heaven, the Father, the Word, and the Holy Ghost: and these three are one. And there are three that bear witness in earth, the Spirit, and the water, and the blood: and these three agree in one." 1 John 5:7-8

• "That he might sanctify and cleanse it with the washing of water by the word, That he might present it to himself a glorious church, not having spot, or wrinkle, or any such thing; but that it should be holy and without blemish ... For we are members of his body, of his flesh, and of his bones." Ephesians 5:26-27, 30

207. WHAT ARE THE RESULTS OF PARTICIPATING IN FOOTWASHING?

☐ Because you've allowed yourself to be humbled, God will exalt you!

> • "For whosoever exalteth himself shall be abased; and he that humbleth himself shall be exalted." Luke 14:11

☐ You will be in agreement with the Holy Spirit, the Restorer, because you will have experienced forgiving your brother, which will cause both you and him to walk in love. By doing this you will realize that you too could become overcome with offense of fault and would need the same act of love ministered to you.

> • "Brethren, if a man be overtaken in a fault, ye which are spiritual, restore such an one in the spirit of meekness; considering thyself, lest thou also be tempted." Galatians 6:1

☐ Those members of the body who have felt rejected will be received, thus "the lame" will be restored to a walk in Christ because of your extended ministry of love and restoration.

> • "And make straight paths for your feet, lest that which is lame be turned out of the way; but let it rather be healed." Hebrews 12:13

☐ You will have been obedient to the scripture requiring us not to do anything in strife, but to esteem our brother and be his servant. Therefore, you will receive the reward suitable for a king.

• "Let nothing be done through strife or vainglory; but in lowliness of mind let each esteem other better than themselves. Look not every man on his own things, but every man also on the things of others. Let this mind be in you, which was also in Christ Jesus: Who, being in the form of God, thought it not robbery to be equal with God: But made himself of no reputation, and took upon him the form of a servant, and was made in the likeness of men." Philippians 2:3-7

Chapter 27
FELLOWSHIP WITH CHRIST
(Communion)

208. WHAT IS MEANT BY THE TERM "COMMUNION"?

☐ The term communion is used to make reference to The Lord's Supper or the celebration of the Passover Feast. Christ instituted the communion on the night before his death. He sat with his disciples and ate bread and drank [fruit of the vine] from the cup. He explained to them that the bread was symbolic of His Body and that the cup symbolized His Blood that would be shed for the remission of sins ushering in a new and better covenant with God. He also stressed to them that the fellowship that they were having at the time was an example and should be done repeatedly in remembrance of His great sacrifice. Today when we partake of communion it should also be done in remembrance of our Savior Jesus. This fellowship [communion or Lord's Supper] confirms the covenant of redemption through the shed blood of Christ.

• "For I have received of the Lord that which also I delivered unto you, That the Lord Jesus the same night in which he was betrayed took bread: And when he had given thanks, he brake it, and said, Take, eat: this is my body, which is broken for you: this do in remembrance of me. After the same manner also he took the cup, when he had supped, saying, This cup is the new testament in my blood: this do ye, as oft as ye drink it, in remembrance of me. For as often as ye eat this bread, and drink this cup, ye do show the Lord's death till he come." 1 Corinthians 11:23-26

209. WHAT IS MEANT BY THE CELEBRATION OF THE PASSOVER FEAST?

☐ The Passover feast was a celebration enacted by the children of Israel, which was commanded by God for them to observe with joy and festivities because He caused their deliverance and exodus from Egypt.

210. WHAT EVENT ACTUALLY TOOK PLACE THAT USHERED IN ISRAEL'S LIBERATION?

☐ God gave a command. The blood of a slain lamb was to be smeared on the two doorpost and lintel of Israel's homes as protection from the wrath of God [death angel sent through Egypt] because judgment was to be executed against that nation that night. All of the first-born people and animals in the land of Egypt died that night except those protected by the blood on their homes. The blood of the slain lamb on the doorpost and lintel of a house was a sign for "the destroyer" [death angel] to "Passover" and not harm anyone living in that house.

211. ARE WE TO CELEBRATE THE PASSOVER IN THE SAME MANNER AS ISRAEL DID?

☐ No. Christ became our Passover lamb. This is what he confirmed at the Last Supper with his disciples. The shedding of his blood as THE LAMB was to usher in the New Covenant. He was the fulfillment of the Passover. The blood of lambs under the Old Covenant was merely a substitute or type until Christ would come and become the true sacrifice for man's deliverance from slavery to Satan and the bondage of sin. We now have true freedom and life in Christ.

> • "The next day John seeth Jesus coming unto him, and saith, Behold the Lamb of God, which taketh away the sin of the world ... And looking upon Jesus as he walked, he saith, Behold the Lamb of God!" John 1:29, 36

• "And it shall come to pass, when your children shall say unto you, What mean ye by this service? That ye shall say, It is the sacrifice of the LORD'S Passover, who passed over the houses of the children of Israel in Egypt, when he smote the Egyptians, and delivered our houses. And the people bowed the head and worshipped." Exodus 12:26-27

212. WHY SHOULD WE PARTICIPATE IN THE "LORD'S SUPPER"?

☐ Jesus Christ commanded us to do it as a reminder of the sacrifice of His life for our redemption.

• "After the same manner also he took the cup, when he had supped, saying, This cup is the new testament in my blood: this do ye, as oft as ye drink it, in remembrance of me." 1 Corinthians 11:25

• "And ye shall observe this thing for an ordinance to thee and to thy sons for ever." Exodus 12:24

☐ It's the confirmation of eternal life and the New Covenant made with mankind through the shedding of the blood of Christ.

• "I am the living bread which came down from heaven: if any man eat of this bread, he shall live for ever: and the bread that I will give is my flesh, which I will give for the life of the world. The Jews therefore strove among themselves, saying, How can this man give us his flesh to eat? Then Jesus said unto them, Verily, verily, I say unto you, Except ye eat the flesh of the Son of man, and drink his blood, ye have no life in you." John 6:51-53

☐ Communing unites the Body as ONE in Christ.

• "The cup of blessing which we bless, is it not the communion of the blood of Christ? The bread which we break, is it not the communion of the body of Christ? For we being many are one bread, and one body: for we are all partakers of that one bread." 1 Corinthians 10:16-17

213. WHAT ARE THE SYMBOLS OF THE BODY & BLOOD OF CHRIST IN THE LORD'S SUPPER TODAY?

☐ Thy symbol of the blood of Christ is the "cup". The scripture refers to the "cup" as the New Testament in Christ's blood. The Body's symbol is the "bread". The scripture also refers to the "bread" as the Body, which was given for the remission of sins. The moment we partake of the Body and Blood of Christ we partake of His presence in us to heal, bless, comfort, strength and encourage us.

• "And he took bread, and gave thanks, and brake it, and gave unto them, saying, This is my body which is given for you: this do in remembrance of me." Luke 22:19

• "Likewise also the cup after supper, saying, This cup is the new testament in my blood, which is shed for you." Luke 22:20

214. IS THE BODY AND BLOOD OF CHRIST FOR EVERYONE?

☐ No. Only the disciples in the Body of Christ are to partake of the communion with Christ at the Lord's Supper. Those who are not believers endanger themselves if they participate. The scripture states that any individual partaking of communion, in an unworthy state, will be "guilty" of not respecting the sacrifice of Christ's body and blood. The penalty for this is that they can become ill and even die. Partaking of the Lord's Supper is intended to be a joyful and strengthening experience, holy and serious reserved only for God's children.

• "Wherefore whosoever shall eat this bread, and drink this cup of the Lord, unworthily, shall be guilty of the body and blood of the Lord. But let a man examine himself, and so let him eat of that bread, and

drink of that cup. For he that eateth and drinketh unworthily, eateth and drinketh damnation to himself, not discerning the Lord's body. For this cause many are weak and sickly among you, and many sleep."
1 Corinthians 11:27-30

215. WHAT ARE DISCIPLES INSTRUCTED TO DO "BEFORE" WE PARTAKE OF COMMUNION?

☐ We are instructed by the Lord to closely evaluate ourselves before partaking communion in the presence of God. We are to ask the Holy Spirit to bring to our remembrance anything we have done against the commands of the Lord written in His Word. If we have violated any of God's Laws, we are to do what the scripture says to make reconciliation with Him. If the sin is hostility against another person, we are to go to that individual alone and settle the issue(s) in love first. If the sin is cursing, lying, anger, rash judgment or any other ungodly thing, we are to immediately repent and be determined not to sin in that area again. The scripture declares that if we eat and drink of the Lord's body and blood unworthily [without repentance], we place ourselves in danger to sickness and even death.

• "Wherefore whosoever shall eat this bread, and drink this cup of the Lord, unworthily, shall be guilty of the body and blood of the Lord. But let a man examine himself, and so let him eat of that bread, and drink of that cup. For he that eateth and drinketh unworthily, eateth and drinketh damnation to himself, not discerning the Lord's body. For this cause many are weak and sickly among you, and many sleep."
1 Corinthians 11:27-30

216. WHAT BLESSINGS DO WE RECEIVE FROM PARTAKING OF COMMUNION?

☐ Just as those who eat and drink unworthily receive the cursing of God, we who are worthy will receive His blessings.

We receive divine health, strength, guaranteed eternal life, resurrection and union [fellowshiwith one another and with Jesus Christ.

• "But if we walk in the light, as he is in the light, we have fellowship one with another, and the blood of Jesus Christ his Son cleanseth us from all sin." 1 John 1:7

• "Whoso eateth my flesh, and drinketh my blood, hath eternal life; and I will raise him up at the last day." John 6:54

• "For as often as ye eat this bread, and drink this cup, ye do show the Lord's death till he come." 1 Corinthians 11:26

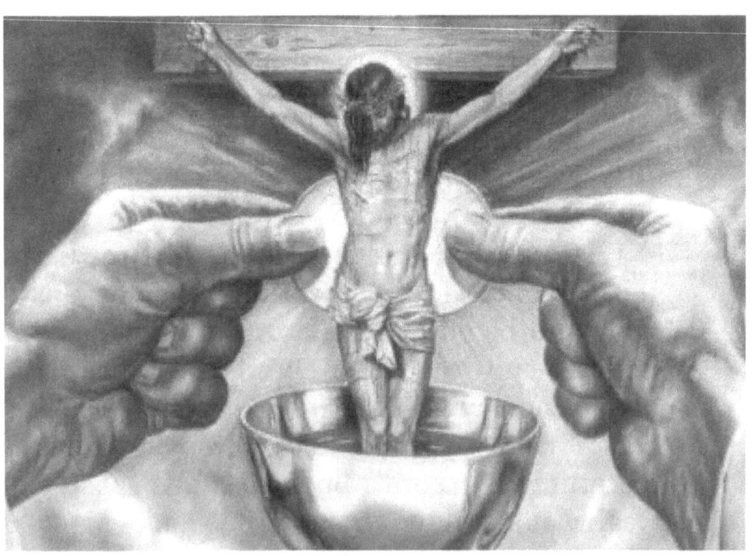

Chapter 28
PRAYER
(Communication With God)

217. WHAT IS PRAYER?

☐ Prayer is talking directly to God. This communication can be verbally or mentally and is accompanied sometimes with lifting hands and expressions of thanks.

- "I will therefore that men pray every where, lifting up holy hands, without wrath and doubting." 1 Timothy 2:8

- "Be careful for nothing; but in every thing by prayer and supplication with thanksgiving let your requests be made known unto God." Philippians 4:6

218. WHAT ARE THE ATTITUDES WE MUST HAVE WHEN WE PRAY?

☐ We must be humble in spirit.

- "When he maketh inquisition for blood, he remembereth them: he forgetteth not the cry of the humble." Psalms 9:12

☐ We must come believing and trusting in God.

- "And Asa cried unto the LORD his God, and said, LORD, it is nothing with thee to help, whether with many, or with them that have no power: help us, O LORD our God; for we rest on thee, and in thy name we go against this multitude. O LORD, thou art our God; let not man prevail against thee." 2 Chronicles 14:11

☐ We must pray in simplicity, expecting to be rewarded of God and not man.

> • "But thou, when thou prayest, enter into thy closet, and when thou hast shut thy door, pray to thy Father which is in secret; and thy Father which seeth in secret shall reward thee openly." Matthew 6:6

219. HOW SHOULD WE APPROACH GOD IN PRAYER?

☐ We should come to God giving thanks.

> • "Enter into his gates with thanksgiving, and into his courts with praise: be thankful unto him, and bless his name." Psalms 100:4

☐ Learn to pray in the spirit speaking in tongues.

> • "Likewise the Spirit also helpeth our infirmities: for we know not what we should pray for as we ought: but the Spirit itself maketh intercession for us with groanings which cannot be uttered. And he that searcheth the hearts knoweth what is the mind of the Spirit, because he maketh intercession for the saints according to the will of God." Romans 8:26-27

☐ Think and meditate on the things you have prayed about rejoicing in knowing that God has sent the answer(s) on the way.

> • "Let the words of my mouth, and the meditation of my heart, be acceptable in thy sight, O LORD, my strength, and my redeemer." Psalms 19:14

☐ Listen to God in prayer. This is a time to allow God to speak to you communication is a "two way" channel.

> • "I will stand upon my watch, and set me upon the tower, and will watch to see what he will say unto me, and what I shall answer when I am reproved." Habakkuk 2:1-2

220. WHAT BLESSINGS RESULT FROM PRAYING IN TONGUES?

☐ We build up ourselves in our faith in God.

> • "But ye, beloved, building up yourselves on your most holy faith, praying in the Holy Ghost, Keep yourselves in the love of God, looking for the mercy of our Lord Jesus Christ unto eternal life." Jude 1:20-21

> • "He that speaketh in an unknown tongue edifieth himself; but he that prophesieth edifieth the church." 1 Corinthians 14:4

☐ The Holy Spirit searches our heart and prays for us according to God's Will for specific situations. This is a benefit because often times we do not know "what" or "how" to pray for\in a situation. The Holy Spirit prays for us in tongues specifically for a situation.

> • "Likewise the Spirit also helpeth our infirmities: for we know not what we should pray for as we ought: but the Spirit itself maketh intercession for us with groanings which cannot be uttered. And he that searcheth the hearts knoweth what is the mind of the Spirit, because he maketh intercession for the saints according to the will of God." Romans 8:26-27

221. ARE WE TO ALWAYS PRAY IN TONGUES?

☐ No. Both praying in tongues and praying in your native language [with understanding] are necessary. It is best to pray with understanding when praying aloud with others. Praying in the spirit is best when praying alone or praying set apart in your own area in times of congregational prayer. This is done to minimize confusion.

> • "What is it then? I will pray with the spirit, and I will pray with the understanding also: I will sing with the spirit, and I will sing with the understanding

also. Else when thou shalt bless with the spirit, how shall he that occupieth the room of the unlearned say Amen at thy giving of thanks, seeing he understandeth not what thou sayest? For thou verily givest thanks well, but the other is not edified." 1 Corinthians 14:15-17

222. WHAT IS CONGREGATIONAL PRAYER?

☐ Congregational prayer is a time when a local assembly or church comes together to offer prayer to God for mankind, God's servants and ministries, special circumstances that affect others and authorities in government. The church comes together as a family to call upon the name of the Lord.

• "Praying always with all prayer and supplication in the Spirit, and watching thereunto with all perseverance and supplication for all saints." Ephesians 6:18

• "I exhort therefore, that, first of all, supplications, prayers, intercessions, and giving of thanks, be made for all men; For kings, and for all that are in authority; that we may lead a quiet and peaceable life in all godliness and honesty." 1 Timothy 2:1-2

223. WHAT HAPPENS WHEN A LOCAL ASSEMBLY COMES TOGETHER TO PRAY?

☐ When a local assembly comes together to pray, God manifests his power. Hearts are drawn closer [unified], the spirit of God is released through his vessels and they will never be the same. Continued congregational prayer strengthens a local assembly.

• "And when they heard that, they lifted up their voice to God with one accord, and said, Lord, thou art God, which hast made heaven, and earth, and the sea, and all that in them is ... And when they had prayed, the place was shaken where they were assembled together; and they were all filled with the Holy Ghost, and they spake the word of God with boldness." Acts 4:24, 31

• "A Song of degrees of David. Behold, how good and how pleasant it is for brethren to dwell together in unity!" Psalms 133:1

224. WHAT IS "PETITION" PRAYER?

☐ Petition prayer is when we go to God with a specific request. We desire something of Him and ask Him according to His Word.

• "And we have seen and do testify that the Father sent the Son to be the Saviour of the world. Whosoever shall confess that Jesus is the Son of God, God dwelleth in him, and he in God." 1 John 4:14-15

225. MUST ALL PRAYERS BE A "PETITION" PRAYER FOR SOMETHING?

☐ No. There are a variety of prayers to be offered to God. Many times we limit ourselves and our relationship with God by using the only prayer we are most familiar with. We should spend time before God trying to minister unto Him through praise, love and worship. In many situations in the scriptures the apostles ministered to the Lord and fasted. God manifested Himself in answer to their verbal and unspoken prayers because He was aware of their needs.

226. HOW SHOULD I RESPOND IF GOD DOESN'T IMMEDIATELY RESPOND TO MY PRAYER REQUESTS?

☐ We must have a continuing attitude of faith in God. God answers the prayers of the righteous! When you pray, believe that you have received them and REST in faith.

- "Therefore I say unto you, What things soever ye desire, when ye pray, believe that ye receive them, and ye shall have them." Mark 11:24

- "Commit thy way unto the LORD; trust also in him; and he shall bring it to pass." Psalms 37:5

- "Therefore I say unto you, Take no thought for your life, what ye shall eat, or what ye shall drink; nor yet for your body, what ye shall put on. Is not the life more than meat, and the body than raiment? Behold the fowls of the air: for they sow not, neither do they reap, nor gather into barns; yet your heavenly Father feedeth them. Are ye not much better than they? Which of you by taking thought can add one cubit unto his stature?" Matthew 6:25-27

- "Be careful for nothing; but in every thing by prayer and supplication with thanksgiving let your requests be made known unto God. And the peace of God, which passeth all understanding, shall keep your hearts and minds through Christ Jesus. Finally, brethren, whatsoever things are true, whatsoever things are honest, whatsoever things are just, whatsoever things are pure, whatsoever things are lovely, whatsoever things are of good report; if there be any virtue, and if there be any praise, think on these things." Philippians 4:6-8

- "Casting all your care upon him; for he careth for you." 1 Peter 5:7

227. WHAT IS TRAVAILING PRAYER?

☐ The Holy Spirit inspires travailing prayer. God prompts us to labor in prayer for our own needs and for the needs of someone else. Travailing prayer employs divine intervention resulting in the change of a condition or person. This spiritual warfare is employed again and again until victory is accomplished.

• "Who in the days of his flesh, when he had offered up prayers and supplications with strong crying and tears unto him that was able to save him from death, and was heard in that he feared." Hebrews 5:7

228. WHAT DO YOU MEAN BY "SPIRITUAL WARFARE"?

☐ Spiritual warfare is actual spiritual battle the spirit of God in the believer against the forces of evil. God has equipped the believer to be victorious in all things. He has appropriated the armor of God for this task.

• "Finally, my brethren, be strong in the Lord, and in the power of His might. Put on the whole armour of God, that ye may be able to stand against the wiles of the devil." Ephesians 6:10-11

229. WHAT IS THE SPIRITUAL ARMOR OF GOD?

☐ The scripture specifies the spiritual armor we have as listed below:

- Sword of the Spirit
- Shield of Faith
- Breastplate of Righteousness
- Truth for Loins
- Helmet of Salvation
- Gospel of Peace for the Feet

• "Put on the whole armour of God, that ye may be able to stand against the wiles of the devil .... Stand therefore, having your loins girt about with truth, and having on the breastplate of righteousness; And your feet shod with the preparation of the gospel of peace; Above all, taking the shield of faith, wherewith ye shall be able to quench all the fiery darts of the wicked. And take the helmet of salvation, and the sword of the Spirit, which is the word of God." Ephesians 6:11, 14-17

Chapter 29
TRUSTING GOD
(Believing In His Character)

230. WHAT DOES THE WORD "TRUST" MEAN?

☐ This word means: to have assured reliance on the character, ability, strength or truth of God; to place confidence in and to commit or place oneself in God's care or keeping.

231. HOW DO WE TRUST GOD?

☐ We must first have had a sincere relationship with Him and have experienced Him as being God and Truth. From this basis we truth wholly in His character, having assured reliance in the character, ability, strength or truth of God to place our confidence in Him completely and commit or place ourselves in His care and keeping concerning His fulfillment of His promises to us through His Word.

232. WHY IS IT SOMETIMES WE FIND IT HARD TO TRUST GOD?

☐ We find it hard to trust God whom we've not seen because our examples or experiences of trusting those whom we do see and had confidence in [parents, spouses, children, friends, etc.] have sometimes violated our confidence in them. These negative results are because of the sin and iniquity in our lives. If we've had negative experiences with those whom we love and see physically it makes it harder to trust and have faith and confidence in a divine God whom we cannot see. Only the Holy Spirit can prepare our hearts to respond and trust Him even though we cannot see Him and we've had some past experiences where others have violated our trust.

> • "And the LORD thy God will circumcise thine heart, and the heart of thy seed, to love the LORD thy God with all thine heart, and with all thy soul, that thou mayest live." Deuteronomy 30:6

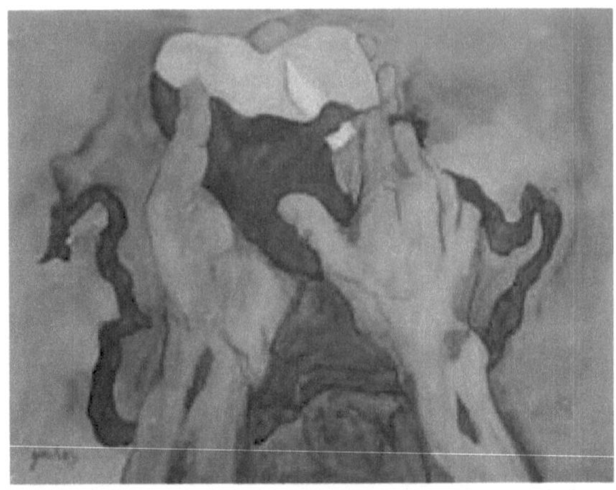

• "And I will sanctify my great name, which was profaned among the heathen, which ye have profaned in the midst of them; and the heathen shall know that I am the LORD, saith the Lord GOD, when I shall be sanctified in you before their eyes. For I will take you from among the heathen, and gather you out of all countries, and will bring you into your own land. Then will I sprinkle clean water upon you, and ye shall be clean: from all your filthiness, and from all your idols, will I cleanse you. A new heart also will I give you, and a new spirit will I put within you: and I will take away the stony heart out of your flesh, and I will give you an heart of flesh. And I will put my spirit within you, and cause you to walk in my statutes, and ye shall keep my judgments, and do them. And ye shall dwell in the land that I gave to your fathers; and ye shall be my people, and I will be your God." Ezekiel 36:23-28

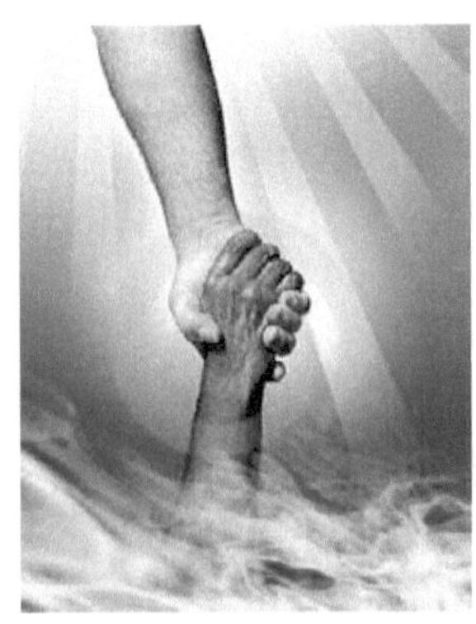

Chapter 30
TITHING OR GIVING
(Your 10% or "What"?)

233. WHAT IS THE "TITHE"?

☐ A tithe is a tenth of your gross financial resources. It's the percentage amount of money God required Israelites to bring to the Tabernacle priests. A tenth [10%] of the 

gross amount of their crops, earnings and possessions were to be set aside by the head of each family and recognized as holy unto the Lord. This meant that one tenth of all they received in harvest; income and gifts [their increase] belonged to God.

• "And all the tithe of the land, whether of the seed of the land, or of the fruit of the tree, is the Lord's: it is holy unto the Lord." Leviticus 27:30

234. WERE THERE PERSONAL BENEFITS TO TITHING?

☐ Yes, they received abundance as they gave.

• "There is that scattereth, and yet increaseth; and there is that withholdeth more than is meet, but it tendeth to poverty. The liberal soul shall be made fat: 

and he that watereth shall be watered also himself." Proverbs 11:24-25

☐ Eternal inheritance into the kingdom was theirs.

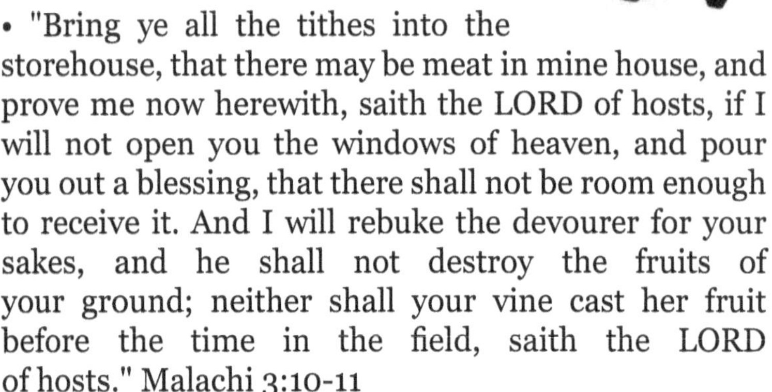

> • "Laying up in store for themselves a good foundation against the time to come, that they may lay hold on eternal life." 1 Timothy 6:19

☐ The evil one was silenced and held back from them.

> • "Bring ye all the tithes into the storehouse, that there may be meat in mine house, and prove me now herewith, saith the LORD of hosts, if I will not open you the windows of heaven, and pour you out a blessing, that there shall not be room enough to receive it. And I will rebuke the devourer for your sakes, and he shall not destroy the fruits of your ground; neither shall your vine cast her fruit before the time in the field, saith the LORD of hosts." Malachi 3:10-11

☐ Their lives showed forth the fruit of righteousness.

> • "Now he that ministereth seed to the sower both minister bread for your food, and multiply your seed sown, and increase the fruits of your righteousness." 2 Corinthians 9:10

☐ Abundant blessings were to be poured upon the tither.

> • "Bring ye all the tithes into the storehouse, that there may be meat in mine house, and prove me now herewith, saith the LORD of hosts, if I will not open you the windows of heaven, and pour you out a blessing, that there shall not be room enough to receive

it. And I will rebuke the devourer for your sakes, and he shall not destroy the fruits of your ground; neither shall your vine cast her fruit before the time in the field, saith the LORD of hosts." Malachi 3:10-11

235. WHAT ARE THE SPECIFIC BLESSINGS OF TITHING ACCORDING TO SCRIPTURE?

☐ The word of God states in Deuteronomy chapter 28 that if we would do all God's commandments, there will be a place of elevation above the world and blessings will overtake us. The following are specific blessings itemized for a "tither" taken from Deuteronomy Chapter 28:1 15. The word "blessed" in this chapter is translated in the Hebrew as "happy or to be envied."

- BLESSED SHALL YOU BE IN THE CITY
- BLESSED SHALL YOU BE IN THE FIELD
- BLESSED SHALL BE THE FRUIT OF THY BODY
- BLESSED SHALL BE THE FRUIT OF THY LAND
- BLESSED SHALL BE THY CATTLE
- BLESSED SHALL BE THE INCREASE OF THY KIND
- BLESSED SHALL BE THE FLOCKS OF THY SHEEP
- BLESSED SHALL BE YOUR BASKET
- BLESSED SHALL BE YOUR STORE
- BLESSED SHALL YOU BE WHEN YOU GO OUT
- YOUR ENEMY WHO RISE AGAINST YOU SHALL BE SMITTEN BEFORE THY FACE
- YOUR STOREHOUSES SHALL BE BLESSED
- ALL YOU SET YOUR HAND TO DO WILL BE BLESSED
- YOU SHALL BE BLESSED IN THE LAND
- YOU SHALL BE ESTABLISHED HOLY UNTO GOD
- THE PEOPLE OF EARTH SHALL SEE YOU ARE CALLED BY GOD
- THE PEOPLE OF EARTH SHALL RESPECT YOU
- THE LORD SHALL OPEN UNTO THEE HIS GOOD TREASURE
- THE HEAVEN WILL RAIN UPON YOUR LAND IN SEASON

-     YOU WILL LEND TO MANY
-     YOU WILL NOT NEED TO BORROW
-     YOU WILL BE THE HEAD AND NOT THE TAIL
-     YOU WILL BE ABOVE ONLY, NOT BENEATH

-     Please note that in Deuteronomy chapter 28:16-64 that the scriptures spell out specific "curses" that will come upon the individuals who will not harken to the word of God by bringing their tithes unto the Lord.

236. WHAT IS TO BE OUR ATTITUDE WITH GIVING AND TITHING?

☐ The words "giving" and "tithing" were used with two different Covenants and have two different interpretations from the scriptures. Tithing was under the Old Covenant and giving is instituted under the New Covenant.

☐ This principle of tithing is part of the Old Testament which was a foreshadow of the true principle(s) to be revealed in the New Covenant under Christ's new order. God required tithing. This principle was instituted through the Law or divine commandment by God in order to position mankind in such a way so that He could bless them abundantly.

☐ Under the Law, to tithe, even though it was out of obligation, indicated that an individual was making a spiritual decision [a decree honorable within the spiritual realm] to first and foremost acknowledge, surrender his dependence, and worship God Instead of himself or the enemy [Devil].

☐ Under the New Covenant, Jesus did not speak of tithing but of "giving." Tithing, under the Law, required or mandated 10% giving. Under the New Covenant, God gives all things unto us. God actually owns the whole earth. We own nothing ... we are made as "stewards" or joint heirs to this inheritance. As a result, God wants us to give unto Him from our provisions "willingly" as a response to His divine Love towards us.

• "Now therefore, if ye will obey my voice indeed, and keep my covenant, then ye shall be a peculiar treasure unto me above all people: FOR ALL THE EARTH IS MINE." Exodus 19:5

• "The land shall not be sold for ever: FOR THE LAND IS MINE; for ye are strangers and sojourners with me." Leviticus 25:23

• "THE EARTH IS THE LORD'S, AND THE FULNESS THEREOF; THE WORLD, AND THEY THAT DWELL THEREIN." Psalms 24:1

• "FOR EVERY BEAST OF THE FOREST IS MINE, and the cattle upon a thousand hills." Psalms 50:10

• "THE SILVER IS MINE, AND THE GOLD IS MINE, saith the Lord of hosts." Haggai 2:8

☐ As you can see, God owns all the earth, lands, the world, its inhabitants, all beasts and all the silver and gold. The key important point is that He allows us to be His stewards over these earthly possessions.

☐ Sometimes we can be deceived (by having riches) to think that we are not held accountable to anyone for how we manage our finances, but we will be ultimately and eternally accountable to God for our record of our stewardship.

☐ Ironically we have no problem accepting the fact that if we want to own a home that many of us had to obtain a loan of finances to accomplish this. Consider that we are paying monthly mortgage or rent notes in order to live in our homes or apartments today. Maybe in 10, 15, 20, 25 or 30 years from now after making consistent monthly payments, we will get the deed for the property from your mortgagor. In legal terms, you do not actually or singularly own your place of residence. As long as you make those payments, you are allowed by your mortgagor to live and operate in the facility as we wish to do so. If we do not make those monthly obligations, the owner will eventually evict you from the premises. They aren't concerned for your other financial obligations. They know this is a necessity in life and expect you to pay this one promptly. This will ultimately effect the rest of our lifestyle it's a primary need for survival.

☐ God feels the same way about His earth and its properties ... He expects us to give, not to be a money miser (personally He doesn't need it to survive) or to boast of His authority or control (both of which are also His) but to keep us in a place and position where He can bless us. See, the benefits from giving really overwhelmingly benefits and favors us. It serves for us as a constant reminder that we must depend upon The Father God for all blessings and finances and not upon our abilities or ourselves.

237. HOW SHOULD WE BE GIVING OFFERINGS UNTO GOD?

☐ Under the New Covenant, we have access to God the Father through Christ Jesus. It is through Him that we receive all our benefits and inheritance. We do not know of Christ after the flesh because none of us were alive when He walked the earth. We only know Him after the Spirit. We recognize His Voice and Presence by knowing His Word. We've developed in our relationship and knowledge of Him through prayer, fasting, reading and meditating on the Bible; fellowship with other saints and submitting to the local church Christ has planted you in. Let Him tell you where and what to give. In the New Testament, Christ spoke extensively about giving. He said we should give:

- *Cheerfully.*

- "Every man as he purposed in his heart, so let him give; not grudgingly, or of necessity; for God loveth a cheerful giver." 2 Corinthians 9:7

- *Without boasting, but in simplicity.*

• "... He that giveth, let him do it with simplicity." Romans 12:8

• *Voluntarily (without force).*

• "For if there be first a willing mind, it is accepted according to that a man hath, and not according to that he hath not." 2 Corinthians 8:12

• *Bountiful, not sparingly, working in us thankfulness unto God.*

• "But this I say, He which soweth sparingly shall reap also sparingly; and he which soweth bountifully shall reap also bountifully Every man according as he purposed in his heart, so let him give; not grudgingly, or of necessity: for God loveth a cheerful giver. And God is able to make all grace abound toward you; that ye, always having all sufficiency in all things, may abound to every good work: (As it is written, He hath dispersed abroad; he hath given to the poor: his righteousness remaineth for ever. Now he that ministereth seed to the sower both minister bread for your food, and multiply your seed sown, and increase the fruits of your righteousness; Being enriched in every thing to all bountifulness, which causeth through us thanksgiving to God." 2 Corinthians 9:6-11

• "Give, and it shall be given unto you; good measure, pressed down, and shaken together, and running over, shall men give into your bosom. FOR WITH THE SAME MEASURE THAT YE METE WITHAL IT SHALL BE MEASURED TO YOU AGAIN." Luke 6:38

238. WHERE ARE WE TO BRING OUR OFFERINGS?

☐ According to scripture in the Old Testament, we were to take our tithe to the "storehouse". This means the place where we receive our spiritual food and guidance. In today's language we are to bring our offering to the local assembly where we have submitted ourselves to be planted and developed under the hands of godly Leadership.

> • "Now concerning the collection for the saints, as I have given order to the churches of Galatia even so do ye. Upon the first day of the week let every one of you lay by him in store, as God hath prospered him, that there be no gatherings when I come." 1 Corinthians 16:1-2

> • "Bring ye all the tithes into the storehouse..." Malachi 3:10

239. WHAT ARE SOME OF THE NEEDS OF THE BODY OF CHRIST THAT ARE MET AS A RESULT OF OUR GIVING?

☐ Prospering, growing congregations support those churches smaller and less financially secure.

> • "Moreover, brethren we do you to wit of the grace of God bestowed on the churches of Macedonia; How that in a great trial of affliction the abundance of their joy and their deep poverty abounded unto the riches of their liberality. For to their power, I bear record, yea, and beyond their power they were willing of themselves; Praying us with much intreaty that we would receive the gift, and take upon us the fellowship of the ministering to the saints. And this they did, not as we hoped, but first gave their own selves to the Lord, and unto us by the will of God." 2 Corinthians 8:1-5

☐ Outreach support and ministries are supported so that the good news of Jesus Christ can be noised in every place. Outreach ministries are defined as minstries or services, exclusive of the local church, that meet the needs of others [ie. widows, fatherless children and strangers].

• "Notwithstanding ye have well done, that he did communicate with my affliction. Now ye Philippians know also, that in the beginning of the gospel, when I departed from Macedonia, no church communicated with me as concerning giving and receiving, but ye only." Philippians 4:14-15

☐ In Deuteronomy 26:12, scripture says: "I have given unto the Levite, the stranger, the fatherless, and the widow, that they may eat within thy gates, and be filled ..." This scripture text is inferring that we should allocate and support portions of our giving resources, in addition to our offering to our local church, to go to the levites, the stranger, the fatherless, and the widows.

☐ The Law required the people in every community to take a personal interest in the poor and to give them individual encouragement. We are to exercise this same stewardship of our resources. We are to be gracious and bountiful to others, just as God has been bountiful to us.

> • The word "levite" refers to the priests, and workers called to labor in the Temple of God. This would encompass our local churches, outreach ministries, TV ministries, and all true present day ministries of the Body of Christ.

> • The word "stranger" refers to a guest or foreigner who is passing through; someone unknown.

> • The word "fatherless" refers to orphan children.

> • The word "widow" refers to a person whose mate is deceased.

> • "Cursed be he that perverted the judgment of the stranger, fatherless, and widow. And all the people shall say, Amen." Deuteronomy 27:19

• "They break in pieces thy people, O Lord, and afflict thine heritage. They slay the widow and the stranger, and murder the fatherless. Yet they say, The Lord shall not see, neither shall the God of Jacob regard it." Psalms 94:5-7

• "Learn to do well; seek judgment, relieve the oppressed, judge the fatherless, plead for the widow." Isaiah 1:17

• "If ye oppress not the stranger, the fatherless, and the widow, and shed not innocent blood in this place, neither walk after other gods to your hurt: Then will I cause you to dwell in this place, in the land that I gave to your fathers, for ever and ever." Jeremiah 7:6-7

• "Thus saith the Lord; Execute ye judgment and righteousness, and deliver the spoiled out of the hand of the oppressor: and do no wrong, do no violence to the stranger, the fatherless, nor the widow, neither shed innocent blood in this place." Jeremiah 22:3

• "And oppress not the widow, nor the fatherless, the stranger, nor the poor, and let none of you imagine evil against his brother in your heart." Zechariah 7:10

• "And I will come near to you in judgment; and I will be a swift witness against the sorcerers, and against the adulterers, and against false swearers, and against those that oppress the hireling in his wages, the widow, and the fatherless, and that turn aside the stranger from his right, and fear not me, saith the Lord of hosts." Malachi 3:5

• "Pure religion and undefiled before God and the Father is this, To visit (to go see, inspect, select, and look out for) the fatherless and widows in their affliction, and keep himself unspotted from the world." James 1:27

☐ Two words that were used repeatedly throughout these scriptures were "judgment" and "oppressed". "Judgment" was translated to describe the process of doing right, discerning righteousness on behalf of these individuals, even protecting them from false judgment against them. "Oppressed" was interpreted to mean having been afflicted, deceived, robbed and made destitute by another.

☐ Our giving cares for the local church ministry.

> • "As we have therefore opportunity, let us do good unto all men, especially unto them who are of the household of faith." Galatians. 6:10

240. IS TITHING & OFFERINGS NEW?

☐ No! Tithing began in the book of Genesis. Abraham gave a tenth to a priest during his time. This was before the Law of Moses. We were not just to give in the past but also the present times of today.

> • "And Melchizedek king of Salem brought forth bread and wine; and he was the priest of the most high God. And he blessed him, and said, blessed be Abram of the most high God, possessor of heaven and earth; and blessed be the most high God, which hath delivered thine enemies into thy hand. And [Abraham] gave him tithes of all." Genesis 14:18-20

> • "Give, and it shall be given unto you; good measure, pressed down, and shaken together, and running over, shall men give into your bosom. For with the same measure that ye mete withal it shall be measured to you again." Luke 6:38

☐ All that was done in the Old Testament was done for example for us in the New Testament. Remember, Christ came to fulfill the scriptures not to abolish them. Through fulfilling the scriptures and the Law, he established grace and reconciliation for mankind to now have a right relationship with God.

Chapter 31
GOD'S ORDER OF PRAISE & WORSHIP
(In Spirit and Truth)

241. WHAT IS THE DIFFERENCE BETWEEN PRAISE AND WORSHIP?

☐ Praise means: to express a favorable judgment of; to commend; to glorify or bestow honor, admiration, or elevate by acknowledging its perfection and it's an expression of approval of God.

☐ Worship means: reverence offered a divine being or supernatural power; extravagant respect, humbled admiration for or devotion to God expressed by one falling on their face[s] before Him; to highly honor, respect, render devotion and appreciate God in sincere purity of the heart.

☐ Although these two words sound similar the difference between the two is that one attitude follows the other. First one "praises" God and as he gives himself [completely physically] in praise he will begin to "worship" God from his spirit. Worship is a higher and broader extension of praise to God.

242. WERE BOTH OF THESE ATTITUDES FOUND IN THE OLD COVENANT?

☐ Yes. God required both praise and worship from His people. These attitudes were limited in their expression due to the "hardness" of man's heart but under the New

Covenant having circumcised the "old hard heart" through water baptism, man is now able to praise and worship God in spirit and in truth with absolute freedom.

243. TO WHAT EXTENT WAS PRAISE AND WORSHIP FOUND UNDER THE OLD COVENANT?

☐ In the Old Covenant, God was a God who "came upon, surrounded or overshadowed" the believer. Under this covenant, God required Israel to celebrate seven [7] different feasts throughout the year. God required the people, as an act of required rituals, to praise Him. He also required animal sacrifices for the covering of the sins of mankind [the slaying of bulls, doves lambs, etc.]. These sacrifices had to be repeated for each sin throughout the year because man was weak and animal's blood could not remove man's sins, only temporarily cover them.

> • "But in those sacrifices there is a remembrance again made of sins every year. For it is not possible that the blood of bulls and of goats should take away sins." Hebrews 10:3-4

244. HOW ARE WE TO PRAISE AND WORSHIP GOD UNDER THE NEW COVENANT?

☐ Under the New Covenant, we are the actual "temple" of the living God   He dwells within us in the person of the Holy Spirit. In this covenant God is requiring spiritual sacrifices such as the fruit of our lips, thanksgiving, dancing and praise to His name. We are only able to offer these spiritual sacrifices because Jesus Christ one time, sacrificed Himself as THE LAMB for the sins of mankind. The strength of His sacrifice was sufficient enough to completely remove the sins of mankind; therefore, there is no need for any other blood sacrifice Christ thoroughly finished the work! Today we worship God in spirit and in truth He calls it "true worship".

• "How much more shall the blood of Christ, who through the eternal Spirit offered himself without spot to God, purge your conscience from dead works to serve the living God?" Hebrews 9:14

• "By him therefore let us offer the sacrifice of praise to God continually, that is, the fruit of our lips giving thanks to his name. But to do good and to communicate forget not: for with such sacrifices God is well pleased." Hebrews 13:15-16

• "But the hour cometh, and now is, when the true worshippers shall worship the Father in spirit and in truth: for the Father seeketh such to worship him. God is a Spirit: and they that worship him must worship him in spirit and in truth." John 4:23-24

245. HOW DO WE WORSHIP GOD "IN SPIRIT"?

☐ To worship God "in spirit" is to permit the Holy Spirit to inspire your new spirit to trust and cooperate with His unction by praising, loving, adoring and thanking God the Father. Disciples are born again [redeemed in spirit] by the Holy Spirit [breath of God - life]. Worship is when this new redeemed spirit of ours is in cooperation with His Spirit inspiring us to show our love toward God. As His Spirit moves within our spirit, pure worship is sparked from our hearts and ascends to God the Father directly. It's an exciting experience to have a "direct" audience with your Creator and Father this worship will change your life and cause you to seek to know Christ more intimately. Nothing can or should take priority over worshipping in the life of a believer.

• "But he that is joined unto the Lord is one spirit." 1 Corinthians 6:17

• "The Spirit itself beareth witness with our spirit, that we are the children of God." Romans 8:16

> • "To the chief Musician upon Muthlabben, A Psalm of David. I will praise thee, O LORD, with my whole heart; I will show forth all thy marvelous works. I will be glad and rejoice in thee: I will sing praise to thy name, O thou most High." Psalms 9:1-2

246. HOW DO WE WORSHIP GOD "IN TRUTH"?

☐ To worship God "in truth" simply means to worship Him according to the principles outlined in the Word of God. His Word is TRUTH. Scripture describes "how" we are to worship God. There are a variety of expressions acceptable for praise and worship from God's Word, He expects us to express our love toward Him individually. We are to worship in truth according to the standard of the Word of God.

> • "Sanctify them through thy truth: thy word is truth." John 17:17

247. WHAT ARE THE RESULTS OF WORSHIPPING "IN SPIRIT AND TRUTH?"

☐ Divine order of worship will be the result of worshipping in spirit and in truth. Both the Spirit and the Word are needed in worshipping God. Without His presence [God's Spirit] worship is dead and lifeless, without illumination, empty, kills and brings no life   it's the "letter" of the Law. Without the Word [Truth] worship becomes emotional, fanatical, soulish and full of feelings without God's Word used as a guideline for order and godly form. It's the wisdom of God that commands us to worship in both Spirit and in Truth.

> • "God is a Spirit: and they that worship him must worship him in spirit and in truth." John 4:24

248. WHAT ARE SOME EXPRESSIONS OF WORSHIP DESCRIBED IN THE SCRIPTURES?

☐ The singing of praises to God.

• "Sing praises to God, sing praises: sing praises unto our King, sing praises. For God is the King of all the earth: sing ye praises with understanding." Psalms 47:6-7

• "A Psalm. O sing unto the LORD a new song; for he hath done marvelous things: his right hand, and his holy arm, hath gotten him the victory. The LORD hath made known his salvation: his righteousness hath he openly showed in the sight of the heathen. He hath remembered his mercy and his truth toward the house of Israel: all the ends of the earth have seen the salvation of our God. Make a joyful noise unto the LORD, all the earth: make a loud noise, and rejoice, and sing praise. Sing unto the LORD with the harp; with the harp, and the voice of a psalm. With trumpets and sound of cornet make a joyful noise before the LORD, the King." Psalms 98:1-6

☐ Experiencing rejoicing and joy.

• "Rejoice in the Lord alway: and again I say, Rejoice." Philippians 4:4

☐ Great laughter.

• "Then was our mouth filled with laughter, and our tongue with singing: then said they among the heathen, The LORD hath done great things for them. The LORD hath done great things for us; whereof we are glad." Psalms 126:2 -3

☐ Shouting and victory cries.

• "Cry out and shout, thou inhabitant of Zion: for great is the Holy One of Israel in the midst of thee." Isaiah 12:6

    • "To the chief Musician, A Psalm for the sons of Korah. O clap your hands, all ye people; shout unto God with the voice of triumph." Psalms 47:1

☐ Giving thanks.

    • "I will offer to thee the sacrifice of thanksgiving, and will call upon the name of the LORD." Psalms 116:17

    • "In every thing give thanks: for this is the will of God in Christ Jesus concerning you." 1 Thessalonians 5:18

☐ Lifting up hands before God.

    • "Because thy lovingkindness is better than life, my lips shall praise thee. Thus will I bless thee while I live: I will lift up my hands in thy name." Psalms 63:3-4

☐ Clapping our hands.

    • "To the chief Musician, A Psalm for the sons of Korah. O clap your hands, all ye people; shout unto God with the voice of triumph." Psalms 47:1

☐ Dancing.

    • "A time to weep, and a time to laugh; a time to mourn, and a time to dance." Ecclesiastes 3:4

    •"Let them praise his name in the dance: let them sing praises unto him with the timbrel and harp." Psalms 149:3

249. WHY ARE THESE EXPRESSIONS NECESSARY?

☐ In expressing praise and worship we minister out of our heart unto God creating an atmosphere for Him to come and minister to believers as well. God wants to minister to us. Spiritual praise and worship causes us to create a habitation for God to dwell in our midst.

> • "Saying, I will declare thy name unto my brethren, in the midst of the church will I sing praise unto thee." Hebrews 2:12

> • "In whom all the building fitly framed together groweth unto an holy temple in the Lord: In whom ye also are builded together for an habitation of God through the Spirit." Ephesians 2:21-22

250. IS THERE A DEPTH TO SPIRITUAL WORSHIP BEYOND PRAISING GOD WITH YOUR INTELLECTUAL UNDERSTANDING?

☐ Yes. As the Holy Spirit moves upon your spirit and worship is sparked through your understanding [English language]; the union between your spirit and the Spirit of God is in perfect harmony. This union sparks a further direct communion with God in that the spirit filled believer can worship God "in tongues" [a spiritual language unknown to his intellect], which is spoken directly and known by God. This goes beyond the simple mechanics of worship, moving into a full and complete realm of communion between man and His God.

> • "Having therefore, brethren, boldness to enter into the holiest by the blood of Jesus, By a new and living way, which he hath consecrated for us, through the veil, that is to say, his flesh." Hebrews 10:19-20

251. WHY ARE WE TO BE PERSONALLY COMMITTED TO PRAISING AND WORSHIPPING GOD?

☐ We must become personally committed to praising and worshipping God because it releases the power of God in our lives and causes the presence of God to be with us [in our midst]. It also helps us to keep our minds subjected to thoughts like Christ and therefore produces peaceful lives. It provokes the blessings of God upon us. As we give ourselves to God in praise, He gives unto us according to our needs. Praise purifies us; we are made clean as we empty ourselves in God's presence. It's like a washing [spiritually] that takes place as the power of God flows through us. This personal commitment to praising and worshipping God:

• Produces peace.

• "Thou wilt keep him in perfect peace, whose mind is stayed on thee: because he trusteth in thee." Isaiah 26:3

• Provokes the blessings of God.

• "For he that soweth to his flesh shall of the flesh reap corruption; but he that soweth to the Spirit shall of the Spirit reap life everlasting." Galatians 6:8

• Causes God's presence to be with us.

• "He that dwelleth in the secret place of the most High shall abide under the shadow of the Almighty. I will say of the LORD, He is my refuge and my fortress: my God; in him will I trust. Surely he shall deliver thee from the snare of the fowler, and from the noisome pestilence. He shall cover thee with his feathers, and under his wings shalt thou trust: his truth shall be thy shield and buckler. Thou shalt not be afraid for the terror by night; nor for the arrow that flieth by day; Nor for the pestilence that walketh in darkness; nor for the destruction that wasteth at noonday. A thousand shall fall at thy side, and ten thousand at thy right hand; but it shall not come nigh thee. Only with thine eyes shalt thou behold and see the reward of the wicked. Because thou hast made the LORD, which is my refuge, even the most High, thy habitation; There shall no evil befall thee, neither shall any plague come nigh thy dwelling. For he shall give his angels charge over thee, to keep thee in all thy ways." Psalms 91:1-11

• Releases the power of God to and for us.

• "And at midnight Paul and Silas prayed, and sang praises unto God: and the prisoners heard them. And suddenly there was a great earthquake, so that the foundations of the prison were shaken: and immediately all the doors were opened, and every one's bands were loosed." Acts 16:25-26

252. IS SINGING AND MUSICAL INSTRUMENTS ACCEPTABLE TO BE USED FOR PRAISING AND WORSHIPPING GOD TODAY?

☐ Yes. The word "song" translates to mean: songs accompanied by musical instruments, a pruned song, an ode intended to be sung and accompanied by a musical instrument especially the harp. Throughout the Old Testament, believers were committed to using instruments to praise and worship God. It's the same for the New Covenant also.

• "Speaking to yourselves in psalms and hymns and spiritual songs, singing and making melody in your heart to the Lord." Ephesians 5:19

• "In that day will I raise up the tabernacle of David that is fallen, and close up the breaches thereof; and I will raise up his ruins, and I will build it as in the days of old." Amos 9:11

As you can see from these scriptures, a singing and worshipping assembly is one where God's presence will dwell and abide. Let us continue to strive for excellence in being a praise and worship to our God!